HARASSED:

100 WOMEN DEFINE
INAPPROPRIATE BEHAVIOR
IN THE WORKPLACE

HARASSED:
100 WOMEN DEFINE INAPPROPRIATE BEHAVIOR IN THE WORKPLACE

Nancy Dodd McCann

Thomas A. McGinn

BUSINESS ONE IRWIN
Homewood, Illinois 60430

Project editor: Jeffrey A. Krames
Production manager: Ann Cassady
Compositor: Professional Resources & Communications, Inc.
Typeface: 11 / 13 Palatino
Printer: Arcata Graphics/Kingsport

Library of Congress Cataloging-in-Publication Data

McCann, Nancy Dodd.
    Harassed: 100 women define inappropriate behavior in the
  workplace / Nancy Dodd McCann, Thomas A. McGinn.
      p.   cm.
  ISBN 1-55623-796-0
    1. Sexual harassment of women—United States. 2. Sexual
  harassment of women—Law and legislation—United States. 3. Sex
  role in the work environment—United States. 4. Women—United
  States—Interviews.   I. McGinn, Thomas A. II. Title.
    HD6060.3.M33   1992
    331.4'133—dc20   92-3330
                                       CIP

Printed in the United States of America
  3 4 5 6 7 8 9 0 K 9 8 7 6 5 4 3

To the women who unselfishly shared their experiences
—and those who devoted their time and energies
evaluating them—so that all women and men
can create a better tomorrow.

And to Ellen, who lent us her name.

Table of Contents

Preface

Women are upset. Men don't understand why.

During the televised Supreme Court confirmation proceedings, sexual harassment stood on center stage in America. Everyone felt its pinch. A young man asked one of the authors to "tell me everything I need to know about sexual harassment to stay out of trouble. I'm not even sure what they're talking about, but I think I need to know." At that moment, the need for a book became patently clear. The crux of sexual harassment stood out—the vast difference between how women think and feel, and how men *perceive* women to think and feel. Discussions began between the authors. Could we, should we, simply ask women to tell us how they thought and felt? The more we looked for a different answer, the more firmly we knew that our original solution was correct.

The idea of asking 100 women to tell us exactly how they thought, to share their innermost feelings and experiences, began to take shape. Would they be willing to do so? We could only bet on the answer, and we put our money on the women of America. Would a publisher be willing to print the message in a timely manner to assist individuals and companies struggling to find answers? We called Richard D. Irwin, Inc. Were they receptive? Absolutely. They also bet on the women of America. We faxed them an outline. The critical element—could every member of their staff take on an extra book and move it "outside the system," months ahead of normal, to meet the market need? Within a day or two, the answer came: "Yes!"

Then our telephone lines began to burn at all hours; our fax machines rolled. We called our professional friends, our "networks," asking for assistance in selecting 100 reasonable women to meet exactly the demographics of the United States. We called heads of agencies whom we had met. We faxed everyone an outline of the project, the time frames, the publication date. Calls began to pour in with responses. "My daughter has a friend who might have a story to share." "I have found two or three women whom you should call. They could give excellent advice and counsel." We called. Word spread. Women began to call us, "I heard from so and so about your book and I want to talk to you about . . . ."

We spoke with the women. Some were hesitant when we first called, and we offered to call back, to let them think about whether they would share their innermost experiences. Many called back on their own. Some began pouring out the hurt and anger stored inside, sometimes faster than we could write. Some were plainly excited about the book and honored to be among the 100 women selected. The file folder of stories began to swell. Soon the list of women mounted—50, 60, 70 . . . 100!

A month later, we knew we had a book—a tiger by the tail. Could we meet our own deadlines? Sixteen-hour days, whirring fax machines and telephone conversations long into the night became our daily regimen. The scenarios were finished, printed on 17 pages, and mailed. We asked for a two-week turnaround. By mail, by fax and by overnight carriers, the women came through.

Survey participants were presented with 50 scenarios of events that have actually happened in the workplace in recent years, followed by the following request for their feedback on each scenario.

Action is: ___Inoffensive   ___Offensive

   (circle to what degree; 10 =high)   1 2 3 4 5 6 7 8 9 10
I feel: __ pleased   __ annoyed   __ used to it   __ puzzled
           __ frustrated   __ angry   __ intimidated   __ degraded
If offensive, actions you would take:

  __Ignore

  __Discuss with individual

  __Discuss with friend/peers

  __Discuss confidentially with member of management

  __Lodge formal complaint to EEO or a lawyer

  __Quit your job

  __Other/comments:_____

All women who shared their experiences with us have been identified throughout as "**Ellen**," who represents *Everywoman*.

While the jury was out voting, the authors researched. Even though we had strong experience bases in this topic, we wanted to know what we didn't know. We held lengthy discussions to put the topic into historical perspective, to ensure we understood the real impact of sexual harassment on everyone. We contacted firms across the country, universities, and individuals to discuss existing sexual harassment programs.

Analysis of the data in any timely manner would not have been possible without the willingness of Carol Blazek and Gina Shiedlak to work long evening and weekend hours to input data.

The authors carefully read each response—Nancy as they came in and Tom when he arrived in Barrington. In the meantime, we began to outline and draft the remainder of the book. Three weeks later, the authors met in Barrington for five days to analyze the women's selections on each scenario, by each type of demographic data. We began to draft our responses for Chapter 1 and weave the trends into the remainder of the book. We'd stop in the midst and say, "No wonder . . ." as trends began to jump out at us. The 16-hour days continued, but what a high learning experience! We were exhilirated, not tired.

In record time, the text was finished and sent off to Professional Resources and Communications (PRC), a Barrington, Illinois, publications management company, where Patricia Wiggenhorn massaged it and Amy-Mae Miller designed and formatted the manuscript to its camera-ready stage. For us, it took three months of 16-hour days! For PRC, it was one month of steady work—including evenings and weekends—to squeeze our book into their tightly compressed schedule. It just shows what you can do with the women of America behind you!

Who We Are . . .

We met 25 years ago when we shared an office at General Electric Company's Information Systems Division in Phoenix, Arizona. Working for a manager who measured results closely and accepted only one's best, a manager most employees would call (in polite language) "tough," we both learned early in our careers that such managers could also assist individual growth and development. Our manager allowed no one to harass another individual; he allowed each person to be herself or himself. A man before his time, he truly believed that was the way individuals succeeded. This tough manager respected us as competent individuals; we also respected him.

We both moved upward in GE through the ranks in human resources positions and into human resources management. We each grew and learned, often taking tough stands when necessary to preserve the integrity and respect of the individual, ourselves or the managers or employees we served. We listened a lot as we helped employees and managers sort out their workplace relationships. We felt good about our contributions when we saw people grow and work environments flourish.

Our paths crossed several times over the years as we made individual choices for positions within GE. Sometimes we worked together, once one for the other and once we lived in the same neighborhood while employed at different GE businesses. After leaving GE, each of us started consulting practices. It was only natural to continue to keep in touch—sharing information and ideas, and asking for feedback and assistance as we served our new clients.

Nancy Dodd McCann is now President of The Fordham Group, a Barrington, Illinois, consulting firm specializing in assessment and organization of human resources and blending of corporate cultures for growth in today's changing environments: mergers, acquisitions, workforce diversity and international expansion.

Thomas A. McGinn, founder of Thomas A. McGinn and Associates, a consultancy specializing in human resources consulting and training, is an adjunct professor at The University of Virginia at Charlottesville and Piedmont Virginia Community College.

When the media blitz about sexual harassment exploded, we were drawn to respond, even though it meant taking time away from our businesses. We realized that we were in a unique position to present this important topic within the context it deserved. We bring to this challenge our professional backgrounds, our commitment to the respect of the individual and our personal belief that mixed gender professional relationships can work. We have made a moral commitment to continue the work of our professional lives through this book. Thus, we present the findings of our research, our understanding of the law, our experience in the workplace and our recommendations to move forward to bring respect to all workplaces.

Acknowledgments

Presenting a book of this scope with the validity it deserves within a useful time frame would not have been possible without the extraordinary interest and assistance of many individuals. Sincere admiration and appreciation goes to the women who shared their own most intimate experiences in the hopes that others would not have to repeat them. Without these scenarios, our research would not have been possible. We also thank the 100 women who took several hours out of their busy schedules to share their thoughts about the seriousness of the events presented to them.

When we began this project, we did not know if we could find 100 "reasonable women" willing to participate within an acceptable time frame. We did not know how employers would react when we asked their assistance. However, we were pleasantly surprised. Most employers viewed this as an opportunity to begin or continue the discussions now ongoing about this serious topic. They responded with outstanding support as they identified "reasonable women" within their environments who matched the demographics that we needed to validate our survey. We will refrain from mentioning the names of these companies in order to avoid speculation about the identity of the 100 women, but we are indebted to them. We are also indebted to our personal and professional friends and the heads of agencies who recommended women to us.

Before we seriously decided to respond to this challenge, we had to consider the logistics, which included professional assistance. Were it not for Professional Resources and Communications, we would not have attempted this work. Co-owners Patricia Wiggenhorn and Graham Core listened to the idea, gave outstanding advice, counsel, and encouragement, and convinced us that we could meet the challenge.

We could not end our acknowledgments without thanking our spouses. Lois McGinn shuffled faxes back and forth, and took and deciphered messages on a regular basis. Jerry McCann created the computer program to house the data base and analyze the results which arrived from the 100 women. Lois and Jerry provided food for the body and soul and supported us in every way possible, without reciprocal support, as we worked long into the night to meet our deadlines.

Chapter One

"Reasonable Women" Define Harassment

Ellen, a doctoral student at a major university, faced a dilemma in her personal life. When she realized that a decision she was forced to make would slightly alter the schedule she had filed with the chairman of her committee, she felt compelled to share the schedule change with him. Early one morning she visited his office and stated, "I will be two or three days late with the results of my research since I will be moving this weekend."

The chairman appeared concerned as he asked, "Why?

She shared, "I'm leaving my husband because he is abusive."

His retort stunned her: "I'll bet you'll miss the rough sex!"

Ellen faced trauma on top of trauma—not unlike what many women face when thoughtless remarks are flung at them. The committee chairman may have been joking, but his remarks were insensitive and Ellen was not in the mood to receive them. In the process of dismantling her personal life because of abusive treatment, she now faced a potentially abusive man in her professional life. The message she received from her chairman was the last thing she needed to hear. Her professional life, present and future, was in the hands of a man who appeared to believe that she really might like rough treatment. He was at the very least totally insensitive to her needs. What should she expect from him now?

She acted typically. To survive, she could not become angry with him. Angry with herself instead, she wondered why she had shared this information. Her options for dealing with the situation were limited. She had invested two years in research and study to prepare for a full professorship. Practically speaking, she could not afford to throw away this two-year investment. If she stayed in the department, she faced a year of apprehension as this man totally controlled her future. Ellen stayed and finished the work, but the joy of discovery, the joy of sharing with her mentor ideas that reveal themselves as one researches and learns, the joy of her current "job" evaporated. She simply "put in her time, waiting for the gates to open and let her out."

Can a thoughtless remark really cause such trauma? One can only speculate as to whether this remark qualifies as trauma in a court of law, since it has not been adjudicated. The victim sought us out when she heard about our study because she was still hurt and angry. She wanted to bring her experience out into the open so that others would understand what she had gone through.

THE "REASONABLE WOMAN" STANDARD

We've chosen this example to illustrate what the Ninth Circuit, U.S. Court of Appeals believed when it handed down a landmark ruling in 1991: that what may not seem to be offensive to a man can traumatize a woman. The Ninth Circuit used a new standard to define a hostile work environment, mandating that the facts in a case must be viewed from the perspective of a "reasonable woman," not a "reasonable man," when the harassee is female. A Florida court concurrently adopted the same standard. In the Ninth Circuit ruling, the Appellate Court explained its rationale:

> A complete understanding of the victim's view requires, among other things, an analysis of the different perspectives of men and women. Conduct that many men consider unobjectionable may offend many women.
>
> We realize that there is a broad range of viewpoints among women as a group, but we believe that many women share common concerns which men do not necessarily share.
>
> For example, because women are disproportionately victims of rape and sexual assault, women have a stronger incentive to be concerned with sexual behavior . . . .

In summary, the court stated that:

> . . . men may view sexual conduct in a vacuum without a full appreciation of the social setting or the underlying threat of violence that a woman may perceive.

This difference in perception has been summed up in plain language by women who state, "Men just don't get it."

100 WOMEN—WHO ARE THEY?

The Ninth Circuit Court ruling stated, "a broad range of viewpoints do exist among women as a group, but we believe that many women share common concerns which men do not necessarily share."

The real meat of this book was written by the women of America. Promised anonymity, we will not share their individual backgrounds. But demographically they represent American women as follows:

Their Occupations

The 100 respondents are currently employed in the following industries: Advertising; Aerospace; Aircraft/Engine Manufacturing; Airlines; Apparel; Automotive; Ceramics; Communications; Computer Services (hardware & software); Consulting; Cosmetics; Data Processing; Services; Defense; Education; Educational Training; Executive Search; Financial Services; Food; Government—City, Elected Office, Federal and State; Government Contracting; Health Care; Insurance; Journalism; Law Enforcement; Law; Media; Manufacturing—Component, Consumer Products, Controls, Electrical Equipment, Wire; Mining; Office Supplies; Oil; Pharmaceutical; Plastics; Product Distribution; Publishing; Real Estate; Retail; Telecommunications; Transportation; Travel; and Utilities.

They are involved in the following types of work: Accountancy; Actuarial Management; Administration; Assembly; Auditing; Banking; Brokerage; Business Ownership; Chauffering Service; Clerical, General; Computer Programming; Credit Approval; Customer Service; Elected Office; Engineering; Executive; Executive Search; Finance; Food Service; Graphics; Government Staff; Human Resources; Information Services; Information Systems; Insurance Sales/Marketing; Intelligence; Inventory; Journalism; Law; Law Enforcement; Management/Supervision; Management Consulting; Media; Nursing; Outside Sales (various); Physician; Pilot; Procurement; Production Work; Quality Control; Real Estate; Reception; Secretarial; Stock Supply; Teaching; Travel Reservations; and Utility Installation.

Within our work group, **44 percent of the respondents are hourly personnel; 17 percent are supervisory** and **39 percent are other exempt personnel.** "Hourly personnel" include women compensated for overtime worked as mandated by law; i.e., assemblers, customer service representatives, production workers, secretarial personnel and technicians. Supervisory personnel include: business owners, managers and supervisors at all levels of organizations. Other exempt personnel include women normally not compensated for overtime worked; i.e., administrative personnel, computer programmers, engineers, financial analysts, journalists, nurses, outside salespeople, realtors and teachers.

Their Ages

Twenty-four percent of our respondents are 20-29 years old; 32 percent are 30-39 years old; 30 percent are 40-49 years old and 14 percent are 50 years old and older. Twenty-five percent represent minorities, including African Americans, Asian Americans, Hispanic Americans and Native Americans. Seventy-five percent are Caucasian.

Their Geography

The women contacted initially represented U.S. regional demographics, according to their current addresses. However, when they replied with specific demographic data, more than 50 percent had lived in more than one region of the country; about 30 percent had lived in three or more regions of the country and some have lived internationally.

WOMEN HARASSED: 50 REAL EVENTS

The scenarios presented might offend you. They offended the women who chose to share them. The scenarios have been changed where necessary to protect the identity of the individuals involved. As with common problems, scenes such as these may have happened in your workplace. We have no way of knowing this, of preventing any hurt or anger or embarrassment from resurfacing. We take no responsibility for any apparent similarities; we are not nor can we be prescient. However, you have our understanding and our condolences.

As we polled 100 women, we found broad viewpoints and common concerns. Collective responses appear statistically after each scenario. Comments by survey respondents follow.

SCENARIO 1

Ellen had been a clerical employee for several years when she decided to become an apprentice in order to qualify for a higher paying job fixing in-house equipment. She was shy and worried that she would have to go back to the word processing pool and lower pay if she did not perform. As she attempted to fix a piece of broken equipment, Ellen's married male supervisor insisted on betting her that it wouldn't work. The only prize he would bet for was "a drink after work."

The Women Respond

Women Offended: 82%   **Degree of Offensiveness: 4.6/10**

Predominant Feelings Expressed: **Actions Advised:**
57% Annoyed   35% Discuss with individual
18% Used to it   26% Ignore

- It took guts for her to leave clerical work that is a safe job for women. Her threatened male supervisor wanted to make sure she returned.
- Tell him to bring his wife if he wins.
- I need the job and will look for support from my peers. Also, if I make no comment to him he may get the message and quit on his own.
- I have *had* to become less sensitive to such joking.
- Forget the guy and concentrate on learning your trade.

Authors' Interpretation

No one would go to EEOC or quit over this issue, but a large percentage saw it as offensive, and 25 percent would talk with their peers about this. A productivity impact? Women moving into male-dominated environments face several problems. Primarily, men hassle women in an attempt to oust them. To survive, women have had to learn to be insensitive to some male behaviors. As this book will show later, industry needs women in these positions as proportionately fewer men enter the workforce in the 1990s. The training of both genders will be required to retain skilled employees.

SCENARIO 2

Ellen took a position as a sales rep with a large company. At first the field manager to whom she reported was friendly and helpful, but very soon his attitude changed. He let her know that he was "doing her a big favor, helping her out," the implication being that if she were male he wouldn't have to work so hard. He stated that if his help were to continue he would "expect more" from her. When she clearly told him it was out of the question, he proceeded to stonewall whatever she wanted to do. He disapproved orders on technicalities, claimed large orders as "house accounts" for which no commission would be paid and visited her clients without her.

The Women Respond

Women Offended: 100%   **Degree of Offensiveness: 8.7/10**

Predominant Feelings Expressed: **Actions Advised:**
81% Angry   81% Discuss with management
43% Frustrated   36% Discuss with individual
                                         24% Take legal action
                                         4% Quit the job.
                                         0% Ignore

- Proceed from management to EEO to quitting if situation is not resolved. Would not let it last more than one month.
- This impacts her earnings potential because of male manager. The money is her support and possibly a family's. No one has the right to deny her money she has earned.
- Why discuss confidentially? The jerk is out of line.
- I would document everything to strengthen my case.
- . . . This is the most despicable of behaviors—not only personally degrading but jeopardizing the economic well being of Ellen directly.

Authors' Interpretation

Women realize the field manager is totally out of line; he drew the ire of 81 percent. Thus, women voted to fight up the chain of command to correct this situation. No one would ignore this. Only 36 percent said they would bother talking to the offender. Gender embarrassment does not seem to dampen the desire to speak up and fight for one's job. Corporate cultures must adjust to provide entry and upward mobility of women rather than condescension and unequal treatment.

SCENARIO 3

Fresh out of college, Ellen joined a medium-sized consulting company. At a client reception, she spent about 15 minutes speaking with a gentleman who was an alumnus of her college. She then moved on to some of the other clients. After the reception, in Ellen's presence, the managing partner said to one of his associates, "We should put Ellen on Mr. X's account. He obviously wants to f— her brains out." Shortly thereafter, one of Ellen's female peers left the company. The managing partner's comment was typical of others Ellen had heard continually in the first month of her employment, as he stated in front of the staff, "Now we'll have to get another bitch to fill her spot."

The Women Respond

Women Offended: 99%   **Degree of Offensiveness: 9.2/10**

Predominant Feelings Expressed: **Actions Advised:**
76% Angry   39% Discuss with management
47% Degraded   35% Take legal action
          35% Quit the job

- If this guy was the managing partner, I wouldn't waste my time working there. There are lots of companies.
- I would not bother speaking to this pig. I don't know if a foul mouth constitutes filing a lawsuit. If I had to deal with this man on a daily basis, I'd quit.
- No one should have to tolerate verbal abuse in a company or at company functions. It is obvious this is an absolute *no win* situation.
- I would quit after I'd found another job elsewhere. Men like that never change, even if you press legal charges. They just get worse ....
- The company has stated in very direct terms their feelings about women and their usefulness in the company.

Authors' Interpretation

No doubt about this one! As data and comments show, you don't have to pull someone's bra strap to be in deep yogurt! Remarks, not touches or *quid pro quo* requests, rate 99 percent offensive and at a 9.2/10. The fact that the offender is a managing partner causes a higher percentage to either take legal action or quit. There's *no one* they can complain to internally. Employees of both genders understand that upper management sets the tone. How can any company recruit and retain talent in an organization with this type of leader? This management might look forward to a class action suit soon.

SCENARIO 4

A woman of excellent taste in clothes and accessories, Ellen always dressed professionally for her position as in-house legal counsel. Since her office was adjacent to that of her boss, Ellen saw him daily. Whenever she wore a particular tri-colored gold necklace, her boss commented on its beauty and her good taste.

The Women Respond

Women Offended: 4%	**Degree of Offensiveness: 1.9/10**

Predominant Feelings Expressed:	**Actions Advised:**
80% Pleased	5% Ignore
18% Used to it	3% Discuss with individual

- I've experienced the exact type of compliment before. After repeated compliments I eventually felt like not wearing the item.
- There is nothing wrong with complimenting on appearance. I compliment and am complimented by both men and women.
- I would be pleased somebody even noticed and had a *good* comment.
- Would probably suggest he buy his wife/girlfriend, etc. a similar piece of jewelry and compliment his good taste.
- I feel pleased when anyone comments on my good taste.

Authors' Interpretation

Most women accepted the compliment since it was not overdone. This situation clearly shows the value of knowing your audience and acting accordingly.

SCENARIO 5

Ellen and five men sat in a conference room awaiting the start of a meeting. The sixth to arrive, a male, strolled in joking: "I see they caught the rapist who got those three gals—I'd sure like to find out what he eats for breakfast."

The Women Respond

Women Offended: 88%   **Degree of Offensiveness: 5.9/10**

Predominant Feelings Expressed: **Actions Advised:**
49% Annoyed   45% Ignore
39% Used to it   34% Discuss with individual

- These are all-too-frequent moments that women manage to get through and go on with their responsibilities.
- I would tell this bozo in front of the others what a pig he is!
- Rape jokes are unbelievably common in mixed company. Obviously men resorting to this humor have no idea of the offensiveness of the word RAPE. The rapist's virility is not the issue; violence is.
- What steps I'd take would depend on the individual. I've had male friends make offensive sexist comments when around other men. However, when I've confronted them they've apologized sincerely.
- Typical of the *brains below the belt* syndrome.

Authors' Interpretation

A high percentage of women were offended, with a wide range of degrees of offensiveness, as the comments show. The most consistent feeling expressed was annoyance, but women would choose to ignore the remark. One woman created another category; she chose "disgusted." Rape is not a laughing matter. The offender would not have made the same remarks if his wife, daughter or mother had been raped. Behavior such as this cannot normally be abated by policies and procedures. Sensitivity training is required to promote understanding of and respect for the different concerns women face.

SCENARIO 6

Ellen, a 19-year-old temporary office worker, was assigned by a major corporation to assist two visiting managers with a significant project. They were given one large, spare room to use as office space. The two men, in their early forties, engaged Ellen in a running discussion that began with requests for restaurant recommendations and things to do in her city. The conversation turned to her personal life, what she did on weekends, how many boyfriends she had, how good a cook she was, etc. These questions were interspersed with gender/sexist remarks about women's capabilities. Toward the end of the first day, one of the managers suggested to Ellen that she come to their temporary apartment that evening and cook dinner for them.

The Women Respond

Women Offended: 90%   Degree of Offensiveness: 6.1/10

Predominant Feelings Expressed: **Actions Advised:**
48% Annoyed   33% Discuss with individual
27% Degraded   22% Discuss with manager
23% Used to it   19% Ignore

- Because they are out of town, some men feel they have a right to act this way.
- The men were obviously taking advantage of her age and gender. Despicable!
- Wonder how these men would react if their 19-year-old daughter came home telling them this happened to her on the job?
- She shouldn't have answered their personal questions to begin with.
- At that age, and even now to a degree, I wouldn't know what to say. I know what I'd like to say though. I'd go for help to get off the job first, I think.

Authors' Interpretation

The visiting managers overstepped the bounds of social behavior. The women's votes show they do not like sexist comments and propositions. While annoyance rather than anger surfaced, 27 percent of the respondents felt degraded, a deep-seated emotion.

In trying to help these men learn about the town, Ellen unwittingly revealed some of her personal life. She was hardly rewarded for her help. Must women clam up so that they don't appear friendly in case it leads to something offensive later? A tough situation!

Hopefully this book will help men to understand the offensiveness of this type of behavior.

SCENARIO 7

Ellen transferred to a position as a city planner where she met Bob, her only peer planner, and Joe her manager. She found Joe very attractive and visited his office frequently or happened to be at the water cooler when he was there, openly flirting with him. Bob, a single male, found Ellen very attractive and noticed how much she flirted with Joe. He also heard them discuss her fitness program to keep her "terrific figure tight." Ellen loved the attention, laughed at his sexually explicit jokes and told a few of her own. Taking this cue, Bob complimented her often and finally invited Ellen to lunch, which she accepted. Soon thereafter Bob began hanging around too close to Ellen and made her uncomfortable. She declined his offer for further dates. Bob then wrote her a letter telling her he loved her. Ellen advised her boss, Joe, who laughed. She then stated that she did not wish to travel with Bob the following week as scheduled. Joe told Ellen she was overreacting and if she wanted to get ahead she would have to work with Bob who was "a key player."

The Women Respond

Women Offended: 60%   Degree of Offensiveness: 5.6/10

Predominant Feelings Expressed: **Actions Advised:**

29% Annoyed   32% Discuss with individual

23% Frustrated   18% Discuss with management

3% Take legal action

- I would tell Bob I had absolutely no personal interest in him and to back off. Interest in one person does not guarantee or imply an interest in *all* people.
- Sorry Ellen . . . sometimes you get what you ask for. Maybe all three should be reminded that work and personal life don't always mix.
- I'm annoyed with her as much as the men. However, if after speaking with Bob he doesn't curb his behavior I would report this.
- Men are accused of sexual harassment for the same type of behavior as Ellen's.
- This is Ellen's problem with Bob. Leave Joe out of it. I think it's normal to expect them to work it out and continue working together. I see no harassment here by Joe at all—normal office relations which Ellen encouraged.

SCENARIO 7 (continued)
Authors' Interpretation

Even though 60 percent of the women were offended, it is unclear how they chose. Many who made comments believed Ellen asked for this behavior and panned her in their response, yet they did not see this as offensive. A double standard? From the low percentage who would discuss with management, most believed this was Ellen's responsibility to handle.

Probably the most complex scenario in the group, it directly involves interactions, perceptions and misperceptions of three people. Are relationships the responsibility of individuals or managers within the group? How much should managers involve themselves? Regardless of her prior actions, once Ellen told Bob of her desire not to pursue a personal relationship with him, he must abide by this decision and change his behavior. And, according to the law, if Ellen advises Joe of Bob's continuing unwanted attention, Joe must insist that Bob change.

SCENARIO 8

When Ellen, a waitress in a restaurant, stood at the bar and placed drink orders with the bartender, the owner of the restaurant occasionally came up behind her and, shielding his hand from the view of others, "caressed her fanny." She repeatedly asked him to stop, but to no avail. His retort was always, "You know you love it!"

The Women Respond

Women Offended: 100%   **Degree of Offensiveness: 9.0/10**

Predominant Feelings Expressed: **Actions Advised:**
82% Angry   67% Quit job
51% Degraded   41% Take legal action

- Before I left (there are lots of restaurants), I would let everyone in the bar know very loudly *why* I was leaving and would spread the word to friends, etc., not to frequent that place.
- With the offender the boss, she has no alternative but to get legal aid and file a complaint. She will probably have to leave her position, but not before she takes action.
- Waitress positions are plentiful enough that no one has to be pawed unless they do indeed *love it*. Wake up women! Sometimes we are our own worst enemies!
- Hopefully by talking with her peers she will find other waitresses who have endured the same treatments from the restaurant owner and can support her complaint.
- Turn around and pinch his —— *HARD*!!!!

Authors' Interpretation

Tips for restaurant owners: Today's woman focuses on earning a living rather than looking for a man to support her. "Hell hath no fury like a woman scorned" has been replaced with "Hell hath no fury like a woman pawed." Modern women understand that it's okay to show anger. Women voted loud and clear to fight fire with fire, crudeness with crudeness. Expect verbal and physical retaliation—and legal action.

SCENARIO 9

A tax accountant in a major public accounting firm, Ellen hoped someday to become a partner at a salary of $300,000 to $500,000. Her male manager, who was generally quite verbal and a bore to everyone, regularly commented about her in front of others with phrases like, "That's a beautiful briefcase you have. Your husband is really taking good care of you, isn't he?"

The Women Respond

Women Offended: 73%   Degree of Offensiveness: 4.47/10

Predominant Feelings: **Actions Advised:**
56% Annoyed   43% Discuss with individual
27% Used to it   34% Ignore

- Talk to the guy. This is way out of line.
- She needs her manager's support to make partner, and this is not offensive enough to warrant making waves and losing his support.
- Only if the comments got out of hand would I say something.
- I could overlook comments, but others could be influenced by these comments, jeopardizing my position. This is another example of bad manners.
- If his comments were unbearable I'd talk to him. Otherwise, ignore. We *all* have to deal with bores in the office, male and female.

Authors' Interpretation

Data indicate a high percentage of offensiveness. However, the number of women who viewed this as offensive went up in proportion to their pay and education, with the highest level of professional women responding 90 percent and the next highest level of professional women responding 80 percent. Unfortunately, some men still think that women are not equal and belong at home having babies, or they dredge up old stereotypes to hassle women competitors. Would this man have made the same statement to Margaret Thatcher about her briefcase? While employers may not be sued over comments such as these, they will not attract and retain competent women employees if this mentality is allowed to persist.

SCENARIO 10

In the assembly plant, Ellen held a pair of pliers in each hand and wired small components to lock them in place. Each component required about 20 seconds of concentrated effort. Occasionally, in the midst of the process, a male co-worker would come up behind her and pull her bra strap.

The Women Respond

Women Offended: 96%   **Degree of Offensiveness: 7.9/10**

Predominant Feelings Expressed: **Actions Advised:**
63% Angry   61% Discuss with management
42% Annoyed   58% Discuss with individual
23% Degraded   20% Take legal action
19% Frustrated   1% Ignore

- One day I'd probably pull up the back of his underwear—that's extremely uncomfortable. And then I'd say, "If you want to be treated with respect, behave like a respectable human being, not the ignorant animal you come across as!"
- I would discuss with the individual. I would also suggest that he be careful where I next clamp my pliers!
- Any blatant activity that interferes in the performance of my job is offensive. If the co-worker had pulled my hair or hand, it would be just as offensive.
- If talking to the individual didn't help, I would go to a trusted member of management, preferably a woman.
- A good manager most certainly would not want disruption of productivity and should handle this for her. Speaking to the offender obviously would not handle it as it should have never occurred.

Authors' Interpretation

Data indicate almost everyone was offended, and to a high degree. The 19 percent response rate toward taking legal action is low considering the potential for success; however, many respondents indicated in the comments column that if discussions with management stopped, they would take legal action as a next step. Expect to see more incidents in the 1990s where women take on this type of offender. Don't expect to see a *wedgie* versus a *bra strap* war. But, what was previously endured as horseplay will be treated for what it really is—sexual harassment and lost productivity. Management can quickly stop this behavior if they observe, listen and take immediate action.

SCENARIO 11

Ellen and her husband, both educators, decided to begin the same doctoral program to prepare to become superintendents of schools. They attended several classes together. For one of these classes, fifty percent of the work was a major research paper on a topic relevant to their anticipated doctoral dissertations. Ellen's husband found little time to work on his project because of unforeseen events in his school district. He gathered rather routine information and analyzed it, turning in a paper he believed unworthy. Ellen, a Phi Beta Kappa with strong analytical skills, worked diligently over the semester to produce a solid work that her husband called a "first-rate analysis." In fact, Ellen's husband told her how much better her paper was than his and how proud he was of her. At the end of the term, Ellen's husband received written comments on his paper, such as, "great job, good information, glad to have had you in class." Ellen received a check mark, which meant her paper was acceptable, no other feedback and a lower grade.

The Women Respond

Women Offended: 78%   **Degree of Offensiveness: 7.0/10**

Predominant Feelings Expressed: **Actions Advised:**
44% Frustrated   57% Discuss with individual
43% Angry   28% Discuss with management
                                             10% Take legal action
                                              2% Ignore

- I've had to some degree the same thing happen to me many times, in less meaningful things, but they hurt just as bad.
- Discuss with her teacher—maybe his paper was more typical of real life—more down to earth. Maybe hers was overdone. No reason to get offended.
- Husband's comments may not have been objective. Ellen should talk to instructor for grading criteria.
- I'd go to the Dean's office with my husband and show the two papers.
- I would petition for an independent review of the grading unless my husband had a strong feeling against this. I might do it anyway . . .

SCENARIO 11 (continued)
Authors' Interpretation

An interesting situation in that grading can be very subjective and any bias would be difficult to prove. Yet, only 2 percent were willing to ignore this situation. The comments indicate a wide variety of options. A perception exists among college students and graduates that some professors believe they were given the right to arrogance in the Constitution. Today's woman is learning to speak up and insist upon equality at a very young age. She will surface blatant bias, actual or perceived. She will also be grading schools. Academics must learn to adjust their attitudes if they wish to retain students; i.e., a major source of funds for their paychecks and research, especially in the face of funding cuts by federal and state governments.

SCENARIO 12

Ellen was the only female electrician working for a large construction company that specialized in renovating buildings. During the renovation of an abandoned office building, she was stringing wires through the ceiling to her partner, not visible to her. While on the ladder, Ellen's supervisor entered the room, climbed up on the ladder behind her and fondled her breasts.

The Women Respond

Women Offended: 100%   **Degree of Offensiveness: 9.8/10**

Predominant Feelings Expressed: **Actions Advised:**
94% Angry   60% Take legal action
54% Degraded   54% Discuss with management
                                        12% Quit

- After knocking him off the ladder, I would complain *loudly* to management/owner to have this guy replaced and make employees aware of what constitutes harassment.
- Disgusting. I would certainly take the first step with management. Difficult since there were no witnesses to a serious accusation. Maybe she should grab him in the crotch . . . hard!
- Offensive beyond words.
- After I kicked him good and hard I would go see a lawyer and find a better job.
- I would probably have reacted primarily with a slap, kick, etc. instinctively . . . He *may* have awakened in the next state.

Authors' Interpretation

Be assured that no one checked the block "pleased." No one would ignore this, either. With the high degree of anger and feelings of degradation, more than half would go to a lawyer or the EEOC. Most of the participants who chose to comment realized the dilemma of proving an act with no witnesses. Their choices dramatize the seriousness of this abusive act. They are not adverse to using physical force when necessary to combat it. Employers must have appropriate channels for communication and sanctions in place to deter such offensive actions. Sloughing this off as horseplay will only win you a costly lawsuit you will lose.

SCENARIO 13

Ellen's large firm, with a predominantly female manufacturing workforce, decided to offer one week of supervisory training in a different city to potential line supervisors. Carefully reviewing proposed candidates, management decided to exclude single mothers because they "could not understand how the children would receive childcare."

The Women Respond

Women Offended: 90%   **Degree of Offensiveness: 7.7/10**

Predominant Feelings Expressed: **Actions Advised:**
44% Angry   53% Discuss with management
43% Frustrated   39% Take legal action
25% Annoyed

- Single mothers who routinely arrange childcare to enable themselves to work certainly should be given the opportunity to arrange childcare for a week away from home!
- You don't make up my mind for me!
- I would lodge a complaint only as a last resort. I would try to change the system first.
- Help them realize the opportunity is especially important to single mothers and should be offered.
- Management should realize (or be informed) that it may be excluding valuable staff members by making this decision.

Authors' Interpretation

When a woman's paycheck is attacked, mere annoyance fades and anger and frustration surface. Data indicate that management cannot afford to discriminate against single mothers either intentionally or unintentionally. Most participants considered this offensive to a high degree and would take action. Policies and guidelines may exist, but individual managers sometimes make counter decisions because they "know best." These unconscious biases screen out valuable employees and can be doubly costly if you are sued. The number of single mothers continues to grow as a percentage of the workplace. This will continue as welfare dollars diminish and women increasingly are expected to work. Employers might want to perform an in-house audit to determine if this could happen in their workplace.

SCENARIO 14

While sitting at her desk at work, Ellen received a phone call from her husband telling her that her favorite uncle and godfather had just passed away. She knew that he had cancer and had planned to visit him in another state over the next weekend. She did not expect his death so soon. As she hung up the phone, she burst into tears. A vice president of the company passed by her cubicle at that very moment. She did not know him well, but had attended meetings in his office and had chatted informally with him in the hallway. When he asked what was wrong, she told him. Then she started to shake and cry even more audibly. He entered the cubicle and put his arm around her.

The Women Respond

Women Offended: 2%   Degree of Offensiveness: 0%

Predominant Feelings Expressed: Actions Advised:
65% Pleased   1% Ignore
 3% Puzzled

- Pleased that a person in his capacity should show compassion.
- No feeling to describe the above—compassion is not available in many people—a human reaction.
- Compassion for our fellow man is okay!
- Don't be afraid to accept comfort when appropriately offered.
- This would really depend on how it felt to me. Even if not offended by it, I would prefer he *not* do this. An offer of "can I help?" would be more appropriate.
- Vice president seems to be a compassionate person and is offering comfort. I'd hope he would do the same for a male employee.

Authors' Interpretation

Data show overwhelming evidence that consoling Ellen *at that moment* was not viewed as offensive. In every other scenario, women voted to reject bodily contact. Yet here women have accepted it because they voted for compassion rather than bodily contact. In the experience base of most employees, male or female, compassion and humanity are rare in corporate leaders. We should treasure it, and say thank you. Employees of both genders want to believe that leaders in every area of employment really care.

SCENARIO 15

Ellen worked with a group of customer service representatives, most of whom were women. A birthday celebration was held for one of the men. When the cake was brought in, Ellen realized it was in the shape of a nude woman. Embarrassed, she scanned the room—most of her female peers (who had ordered the cake) were laughing. Ellen forced a laugh and continued to smile weakly at the crude jokes that followed.

The Women Respond

Women Offended: 60%   **Degree of Offensiveness: 5.0/10**

Predominant Feelings Expressed: **Actions Advised:**
42% Annoyed   31% Ignore
26% Used to it   31% Discuss with peers

- I can't answer this one very well because I am going through this *every* day and I *don't* know how to handle it.
- If women want to be treated with respect they must do the same for others. It looks like these women like this kind of behavior.
- I find it less offensive when women do and say things which are degrading to women as a whole. Mostly it makes me sad that some women don't see the ideals they are propagating.
- Extremely poor taste, bad manners and clearly no concern for others more sensitive in group.
- Tough because it's important to have good working and social rapport with fellow employees. But, this must be addressed.

Authors' Interpretation

Even those who found this offensive were not shocked. Either they were annoyed or used to it. Data and comments show that many women are offended, but do not know how to handle this situation well because it is so ingrained in organizations. Time is ripe for a behavior change. The mission is not to remove fun from the workplace—God forbid—lots of places could use a good dose of fun. But, if 60 percent of women find this offensive, our mission statements need revision. What appears to be lost on most women, however, is that men are properly embarrassed by such behavior. Few saw this as sexual harassment of a male by females, but it is. A double standard? Are women not as hard on women as they are on men?

One respondent's husband, who read the scenarios as his wife evaluated them, contacted us to say how embarrassed he would have been if this happened to him. Our advice: don't give him a nude cake and then be shocked when he "tweaks" your buttocks. But then, you were *only joking* . . . .

SCENARIO 16

Ellen, a manager of training, and a male manufacturing manager were asked to design a new supervisory training program to be used throughout their organization. As a peer, Ellen had worked fairly closely and successfully with the manufacturing manager on many occasions in the previous two years. They had built a solid working relationship. In a growing organization, they faced limited space and heavy workloads. Ellen knew it would be very difficult to accomplish much during working hours if they remained on site. She lived 15 miles from the office, and it was a tough commute at almost any hour. She also understood the need for quiet, relaxed time to think creatively. When she met with her counterpart to discuss a schedule, he suggested they meet at his house two miles away for an afternoon, assuring her that his wife would be there and would fix lunch for them.

The Women Respond

Women Offended: 4%   **Degree of Offensiveness: 3.8/10**

Predominant Feelings Expressed: **Actions Advised:**
51% Pleased   5% Discuss with Individual

- Rational solution to a tough problem—let's be practical.
- The fact that he mentioned his wife would be home tells me this man wanted to squelch any thoughts of impropriety up front.
- Not offended about working at his home as much as the fact that he asked his wife to fix lunch. Should order out, or better yet meet in a neutral place.
- I would first ask if I could call his wife to make sure she would not be inconvenienced.
- Pleased that a man would show such flexibility and thoughtfulness.

Authors' Interpretation

Most individuals were pleased with this action, seeing it as a solution. The very few who saw it as offensive simply were annoyed and would take no action. The real challenge in building a competitive, sane environment is to build *trusting* mixed-gender relationships in the workplace. Data and comments by the women state overwhelmingly they are willing to trust co-workers without evidence to the contrary. In other words, men are trustworthy unless they prove otherwise. One does not need to visit someone's home to prove this trust, but co-ed work teams, business trips, conventions, and so forth require Platonic nurturing to optimize the synergistic productivity power of both genders.

SCENARIO 17

A clerk in the front office of a small manufacturing firm, Ellen was required to walk to the warehouse often. Cutting through the engineering department saved her several minutes per trip. All the engineers were male; the engineering secretary was female. When Ellen complained to her boss that she didn't feel comfortable going into engineering because of all the nude pictures on the wall, he advised her that it didn't bother anyone else and if it bothered her she would just have to walk out to the reception area and around, circling both the engineering department and the manufacturing plant.

The Women Respond

Women Offended: 80%   **Degree of Offensiveness: 5.5/10**

Predominant Feelings Expressed:	**Actions Advised:**
47% Annoyed	38% Discuss with management
29% Frustrated	27% Ignore
17% Degraded	19% Discuss with peers
17% Angry	8% Take legal action
17% Used to it	

- Nude pictures openly displayed in a work environment sounds like something *Saturday Night Live* would do. Are there really manufacturing firms where such is allowed? Just where is EEO?
- At least the engineering men were not making cat calls at her!
- No one should be subject to open sexual pictures.
- I'd go in at night and take down the pictures.
- I believe the key here is 'required to walk to the warehouse often.' When told to take a long walk around—I would become frustrated and seek help from higher management.

Authors' Interpretation

Most comments were simply statements, such as, "The workplace should look professional," or, "Nude pictures have no place in a workplace." A few women who commented have become so conditioned to this that they would ignore the pictures. But this is 1992! Eight percent would complain to an outside agency. Most women want nude pictures removed and will speak up to accomplish this.

Interestingly, no one suggested that men might be offended by these pictures. Many men can distinguish between fine art and girlie pictures! Managements do not have a *safe* choice in this situation. Litigation is ongoing regarding nude pictures and graffiti. The pictures must go. Taking them down now rather than later is the less costly option.

SCENARIO 18

A male congressman in his fifties came to a coffee break birthday celebration for two employees—John and Ellen—who share a common birthday. Both employees report to members of his staff, not to him. The congressman went over to John, congratulated him and shook his hand. He then went up to Ellen, congratulated her and kissed her on the cheek.

The Women Respond

Women Offended: 34%   **Degree of Offensiveness: 3.2/10**

Predominant Feelings Expressed: **Actions Advised:**
23% Pleased   29% Ignore
18% Used to it   6% Discuss with individual
14% Annoyed

- If it was innocent and in good faith, I would just chalk it up to being old-fashioned but it would still irritate me.
- Depends upon the person. Some people wouldn't offend me.
- Maybe he just considered it polite—proper etiquette . . . but I don't want to be kissed by a stranger—too personal.
- He needs to learn some business etiquette.
- Some males feel this is a sign of respect—although a handshake would have been more respectful.

Authors' Interpretation

The statistics do not reflect the variety of opinions expressed by the comments. While two-thirds of the participants checked "inoffensive," many preferred not to be kissed. The behaviors of men toward women are slowly transitioning from social to business etiquette. Women have shown patience in accepting social rather than business etiquette from "gentlemen" raised in a different era. However, women prefer not to be kissed. Management must alert all employees to practice business etiquette. Age and status will not serve as excuses as we move through the 1990s.

SCENARIO 19

Ellen, a project manager at a large international engineering firm, supervised an all-male team. She possessed a high level of expertise and managed time and workloads well. Her team's reactions annoyed her, however, as they often leered at her, interrupted her with slightly off-color jokes and commented more on her figure than her ideas. Ellen decided to confront them about the issue. They told her, "Hey, Ellen, we're just human beings. When you come to work with your skirt so short, and sit on any piece of furniture handy, don't think we aren't going to try to see what we can see!"

The Women Respond

Women Offended: 84%   **Degree of Offensiveness: 6.4/10**

Predominant Feelings Expressed: **Actions Advised:**
39% Angry   32% Discuss with management
38% Annoyed   30% Discuss with individual

- Change, Ellen—Your staff is letting you know that your demeanor and dress egged them on. Harassment is NOT a one-way street.
- If she's the manager, she better get a handle on managing and let them know that attitude, conduct and respect in the workplace will be considered in job performance evaluation and salary.
- Poor judgment on her part for wearing short skirts. Are men wearing skin tight pants that reveal—you know what? The men were frank and honest.
- I might consider firing or transferring some of these people. She is the boss and should *demand* respect and productivity, nothing more or less!
- She can take control of this situation—earn their respect—let them know the limits—downplay her sexuality—and accept their physical attraction to her.

SCENARIO 19 (continued)
Authors' Interpretation

Who is the offender, who the offended—Ellen, the men, or both? Comments indicate a real 50/50 split.

Based on the way some women sometimes dress, the male co-author of this book wonders at times if he is at a cocktail party or at work. The female co-author fully believes women no longer must dress in drab suits like men to be taken seriously. However, flaunting anything is always in poor taste. How we dress and act create our image. If women wish business etiquette in the workplace, should we not wear business apparel? Even office "casual day" requires appropriate, nonprovocative dress.

Does outright provocative dress in the workplace constitute sexual harassment of males or other females by females, just as girlie pictures on the wall and cakes with nude women on the top? Is it really inviting "unwelcome" attention? There is no shortage of room for both genders to clean up their acts regarding dressing and ogling.

SCENARIO 20

Ellen was the third woman to join a 25-person work group respon-sible for electrical utility line repair. Standard attire was jeans and t-shirts. Ellen was well-endowed, with a great figure. When the group assembled for work each day in a fenced-in area at the side of the building, one of the men would routinely see how close he could come to Ellen without touching and how close he could spit next to her without hitting her, as he made remarks such as, "Now I know why we let broads in!"

The Women Respond

Women Offended: 98%   Degree of Offensiveness: 7.7/10

Predominant Feelings Expressed: **Actions Advised:**
62% Angry   71% Discuss with management
38% Degraded   40% Discuss with individual
38% Annoyed   12% Take legal action

- The man is a pig and should be harshly reprimanded and censured, but "standard attire" does not mean it has to be skin-tight. Jeans and t-shirts can be pretty sexless depending on fit.
- He's too sick to confront. I would report him, then go to EEO.
- I'd probably spit on him and say, "Now I know why they let apes in!"
- It's obvious this behavior is meant to force Ellen to quit. Because this inappropriate behavior is sanctioned by the lack of response from management, she must react immediately.
- Some men treat women like a piece of meat. A woman should be able to work alongside of men and be treated with respect.

Authors' Interpretation

Women were not used to or puzzled by this very offensive behavior. Only 1 percent would quit the job over it. The rest are going to fight back by talking with management, the individual and/or seeking legal advice. The law and the reality of the workforce dictate action. Management must (1) sanction the offender appropriately, and (2) initiate immedi-ately a cultural revolution that encourages, welcomes and facilitates women's acceptance into male-dominated occupations. Management has no choice. Hostile workplaces are illegal; women and minorities comprise the majority of the new workforce.

SCENARIO 21

Ellen's investment banking firm held a management meeting billed as a bonding experience out-of-town at a major hotel. When she and the few other women present heard through the grapevine that there was a party in one of the hotel suites that evening, they decided to attend. Stopped at the door, they were advised that they "might prefer to find their own recreation for the evening, which they could do at any price and put it on an expense account." The women chose to enter the hotel suite and found a party in progress, complete with sexually explicit pornography and live models.

The Women Respond

Women Offended: 76%   **Degree of Offensiveness: 7.0/10**

Predominant Feelings Expressed: **Actions Advised:**
35% Annoyed   35% Discuss with Management
29% Angry   25% Ignore
27% Degraded   21% Discuss with peers
                                           12% Take legal action

- Leave the party after a short while—make an appearance—don't let them intimidate you.
- They were never invited and should not have crashed the party.
- What people do in their private time is not my concern. However, if this party were paid for by the company I'd report it. The bribe to put their recreation on expense account is offensive and unethical.
- This is tricky. Some might consider this personal time which is their own business. Entertainment should have been provided for all.
- This type of scenario contributes to the glass ceiling, which is one of the most heinous manifestations of discrimination.

Authors' Interpretation

The women were warned; company funds may or may not have paid for the pornography and models; and, the nature of the party, regardless of who paid for it are key points. The net result is that 24 percent of the respondents did not see this as offensive. These who did were more than mildly upset. Women also indicated that they would not even vent their anger to the individuals. They would advise management and peers.

Events such as these contribute to the corporate image, good or bad. A corporate image impacts recruiting, retention of employees, and consumer purchasing power.

SCENARIO 22

Ellen took a temporary secretarial position with a firm to fill in for a woman on maternity leave. She worked with a group of males aged 35 to 45 who regularly made sexist remarks, alluded to their "scores," and talked about "breaking free" and "starting over." Leaving work in the evening about two weeks after she started, Ellen met the personnel manager in the elevator. When asked how she liked the position, Ellen retorted, "It's okay if you don't mind working with men going through mid-life crises." Ellen then exited the elevator at the next floor, thinking no more about it. Apparently she had been overheard by a senior manager of the firm. Just before lunch the following morning, the personnel manager found Ellen in the file room. In the presence of several other women, it was suggested that Ellen "wasn't going to be fired, but had better come back from lunch with a much better attitude and behave herself in a civilized manner."

The Women Respond

Women Offended: 93%   **Degree of Offensiveness: 6.9/10**

Predominant Feelings Expressed: **Actions Advised:**
46% Angry   26% Quit
34% Annoyed   23% Discuss with individual
23% Frustrated   23% Discuss with management
                                     15% Take legal action

- He was angry because of what she said about them, but it's okay for them to degrade women!
- Ellen should have been more specific than labeling "mid-life" crisis. However, the Personnel Manager's retort was completely unfair.
- This is a misunderstanding. I'd make sure this was cleared up.
- If this was recorded as "poor attitude" on personnel records, she should lodge a formal complaint. She learned a lesson in life.
- This company is corrupt from within. Leave as soon as you can.

Authors' Interpretation

Women chose a simple solution to this scenario. As a temporary employee, who needs this hassle? An employee has to prove herself innocent. Even though 95 percent found this offensive, one-fourth of the women chose to leave the company and move on. Ten percent, however, would seek legal or agency advice. Retorting in public doesn't pay. However, management cannot excuse its actions here. Guilty until proven innocent??

SCENARIO 23

Ellen, a mid-level manager in a Fortune 100 company, accompanied seven male executives to an out-of-town meeting. Some of the men were her peers; some were senior to her in the company. At the airport gate, in the presence of the entire party and other passengers, one of the males, not in the same division of the company as Ellen, but at a more senior level, asked her to "stand up." She replied, "Why would I want to do that?" He stated again, "Stand up. I want to see your fanny."

The Women Respond

Women Offended: 99%   **Degree of Offensiveness: 8.0/10**

Predominant Feelings Expressed: **Actions Advised:**
59% Angry   43% Discuss with individual
49% Degraded   40% Discuss with management
                                           17% Take legal action

- Absolutely not—smack him good!
- I would not have been able to handle this at all. I'm sure I would have turned beet red and unable to move and I'm not sure I would have been able to go higher up to management for fear of it happening again.
- Keep in mind—you need your job, you have mortgage payments, kids in school, etc.
- Not only would I stand up, I'd probably tell the bastard to kiss my ass!
- I'd tell him to unzip his pants!

Authors' Interpretation

Data suggest that this degrading remark is taken as seriously as a threatening remark, perhaps because it is. The manager is senior to Ellen in the organization. Only 18 percent of the women would ignore this incident. Another 17 percent would seek outside legal or agency assistance, whether or not they have a case. Again we see an increase in women's self-esteem. No longer will insults be acceptable. The comments show how offensive a remark can be. The only real option a woman has is not to dignify the remark and hope her male peers are as embarrassed as she is. However, anger is hard to control. A woman should never have to face this no-win situation, especially with a manager senior to her. One woman commented that she would be "unable to go higher up to management." Would she have the same fears in your workplace? If so, the culture needs a change.

SCENARIO 24

Ellen worked as a business analyst for a firm of 200 employees that sold services to clients. Half of the employees were accountants and business analysts and 20 percent of them were female. The other half, almost all female, were clerical employees. At the end of the year, the vice president sent flowers to all of the women but none of the men in the organization with a note that read, "Thank you for all your help this year. You gals really do a good job for us."

The Women Respond

Women Offended: 60%   **Degree of Offensiveness: 3.8/10**

Predominant Feelings Expressed: **Actions Advised:**
34% Annoyed   26% Ignore
23% Used to it   16% Discuss with individual
17% Pleased   16% Discuss with management

- Doesn't hurt to plant a seed. Perhaps someday we will be co-workers instead of *gals.*
- It's offensive in that no males got anything.
- I'd wonder if there was equal pay for equal work!
- I like flowers as a token of appreciation anytime from anyone.
- If ignorance is bliss, this is one happy man.

Authors' Interpretation

While 40 percent found the flowers and note inoffensive, most saw the action as outdated. It just doesn't fit the 1990s culture. This held true across all levels of women in organizations. No one would quit, but some would talk to him and/or management. Men with excellent intentions but outdated ideas need to understand their audiences today. Women would like business, not social etiquette. This book is intended to help men better understand how women today think and feel.

SCENARIO 25

Ellen really liked her job as customer service manager for a financial services firm. For several weeks she had dated a manager from another branch whom she had met at a company meeting. The more time she spent with him, however, the more she realized how self-centered he really was and she no longer wished to continue the relationship. She advised him that she would not see him any longer. He found it hard to take no for an answer and proceeded to beg her for a date every day via a message sent through the company electronic mail system.

The Women Respond

Women Offended: 71%   **Degree of Offensiveness: 3.8/10**

Predominant Feelings Expressed: **Actions Advised:**
75% Annoyed   57% Discuss with individual
23% Frustrated   16% Ignore

- Tell him your boss screens all E-Mail to verify business content—or print it and tell him you'll be forced to send a copy to his manager.
- This is a personal matter. The guy has to grow up and get a life. It's a good reason not to date anyone you work with.
- Ignore the man. He will go away finally.
- I would tell the male manager to stop wasting company resources.
- Find a way to block his messages.

Authors' Interpretation

Data imply that mid-level professional women found this more offensive than other populations. Two common responses to this event: don't date co-workers, and ignore him and he'll go away. As some of the comments indicate, many women see this as a personal issue: a break up of a consensual arrangement. When women and men become attracted to each other in the location where they spend the majority of their time, they will probably continue choosing to mix their business and personal lives. Consensual breakups will continue to occur. Hopefully both women and men will see the value of breaking up quickly, effectively and without the involvement of others. However, if one of the parties persists when the other says "no more," management must be ready and able to eliminate the harassment. The law is quite clear on this.

SCENARIO 26

For two years, Ellen had been a manager in a services firm. Her office was located adjacent to the financial analyst 15 years her junior who supported her operation. They had an easygoing relationship in spite of the age difference and her senior position, occasionally having lunch in the company cafeteria and talking about his career. After the company Christmas party, held downtown in a major city, he offered to walk her home—about six blocks—since he had just missed his train to the suburbs. The weather was mild with snow just starting to fall and the city looked beautiful. Knowing that she could not enjoy this without a male escort for safety, Ellen accepted and thanked him. When he reached her apartment building, he invited himself up. She declined, saying he would miss his train and his wife would worry. He then told her his wife did not expect him to come home. Asked where he planned to stay, he stated, "With you."

The Women Respond

Women Offended: 76%   **Degree of Offensiveness: 6.0/10**

Predominant Feelings Expressed: **Actions Advised:**
45% Annoyed   66% Discuss with individual
28% Angry   8% Ignore
18% Puzzled

- Again, personal. Tell the guy to grow up and buzz off and chalk it off to a holiday mood. At work, ignore that it had ever happened.
- Pretty presumptuous. Tactfully decline and send him home. Try to salvage the working relationship if possible. Did you lead him on?
- Never encourage anyone by even consenting to a walk home.
- Here again, I don't consider this sexual harassment . . . .more like mixed signals that should be openly nipped in the bud.
- Clearly state reasons, using best sensitivity possible.

Authors' Interpretation

No one suggested inviting him to stay. Two-thirds would tell him no in some way and close the door. The fact that 18 percent view his comments as puzzling suggest concerns: Is he really serious? Joking? Checking his batting average? This is a delicate situation. Overwhelmingly, women voted to be sensitive, use diplomacy and candor and salvage the working relationship. Mixed signals and/or the holiday mood might have played a part in this event. Our respondents' collective advice: get a good night's sleep and forget it back at the office. That's our advice, too.

SCENARIO 27

Ellen was standing in the hallway outside her office having a business conversation with a married male associate. A manager from another department walked by and loudly proclaimed: "That's who you should be hitting on, Ellen. He's a real stud."

The Women Respond

Women Offended: 93%   **Degree of Offensiveness: 5.7/10**

Predominant Feelings Expressed: **Actions Advised:**
54% Annoyed   54% Discuss with individual
31% Angry   36% Ignore
 0% Pleased

- On any given day, these comments are made by management.
- This guy is a jerk with bad judgment. If comments continued, talk to his manager informally.
- Tell him he is out of line.
- An obnoxious comment right back at him usually does the trick to shut a man up.
- A boor is a boor . . . .

Authors' Interpretation

While the number of women offended was high, the level of offensiveness was clearly lower with most women reporting "merely annoyed." Thirty-six percent chose to ignore the action altogether. Women apparently realize the difficulty of trying to reform "jerks." But, jerks abound. Hopefully their peers will see them as such. As individuals in the workplace learn greater respect for one another, perhaps "jerks" like these will begin to see themselves for what they really are. In the meantime, women have stated they will help this process by speaking to them, either privately or in front of others, with or without embarrassing them in return.

SCENARIO 28

Ellen joined an advertising firm to promote and sell advertising primarily directed toward women. All the other members of her "team" were male. Team members discussed the campaign and the men freely expressed their opinions, often loudly and aggressively. When Ellen believed the advertising would not appeal to women and attempted to present this viewpoint, she was usually overridden. If she proceeded further after this and attempted to give her viewpoint the weight she believed it deserved, she was usually called an "aggressive bitch."

The Women Respond

Women Offended: 99%   **Degree of Offensiveness: 7.0/10**

Predominant Feelings Expressed: **Actions Advised:**
54% Angry   60% Discuss with management
49% Frustrated   39% Discuss with individual

- I've always been amazed/stymied that men were *assertive* while women were aggressive. I'd want to ask them why they were so threatened by me.
- I could not work where I was not taken seriously and treated with respect. If the situation did not improve, I'd quit and contact EEO.
- Discuss at individual level the validity of the ideas. If you can show them you are right once, it may change team dynamics in the future.
- Call them on it and stand your ground.
- I'd express how I felt about their loud and aggressive behavior and explain. . . It sounds like you (men) are intimidated and unsure of yourselves, otherwise we'd deal with the issues . . . .

Authors' Interpretation

Seven percent of the women were merely annoyed. Ninety-three percent suggested stronger feelings. Only 1 percent would ignore this situation. Eight percent would consult an agency or a lawyer, and 12 percent would quit. All the highest paid, most senior people in the survey would quit. This does not portend well for retention of key employees. The vote indicates this is a serious problem. Not upset because someone is ogling or touching them, women find their income threatened. In addition, they are not treated as competent, as equals working on a project. The authors advise use of the *divide and conquer rule* suggested by one of the respondents. Scenarios show that when in a group, most men will not vary from the norm and defend women. Try to reach them one by one and build individual relationships through sharing a wide range of ideas. Then perhaps, yours will be more acceptable and you will not be shut out of the process.

SCENARIO 29

Ellen joined a small investment firm as a stock analyst. Her male manager often took his staff of five men, Ellen and one other woman analyst to the executive dining room for lunch. As he entered, he always joked loudly, "I'm working on wife number three."

The Women Respond

Women Offended: 61%   Degree of Offensiveness: 4.0/10

Predominant Feelings Expressed: **Actions Advised:**
50% Annoyed   39% Ignore
25% Used to it   24% Discuss with individual

- Who cares? A lot of people are jerks!
- I'm annoyed that this image of me is being presented to other executives and co-workers.
- The male manager seems to be embarrassed and unable to handle a female on his staff and to treat her fairly.
- The comment should not be dignified.
- The future wife #3 has my condolences.

Authors' Interpretation

This manager is no doubt carrying some excess baggage. He doesn't understand that the business lunch differs from the social lunch, so he inappropriately refers to it as a "dating game." Women are showing tolerance he may not deserve. They no doubt understand that changing cultural attitudes takes time. It appears that enough women (24 percent) will start *nudging* him to move that process along.

SCENARIO 30

Ellen, a trainee customer service clerk, learned the computer program in her CRT while on the job. When she needed assistance to the next step, her male supervisor provided this, resting his hand on her shoulder as he leaned over to see the screen.

The Women Respond

Women Offended: 48%   **Degree of Offensiveness: 3.1/10**

Predominant Feelings Expressed: **Actions Advised:**
34% Annoyed   36% Discuss with individual
23% Used to it   19% Ignore

- Immediately remove his hand; if he persists, stand up and let him sit.
- If that's all, no big deal.
- Not necessary to have bodily contact to learn CRT.
- I would try to finesse this situation if possible—offer him a chair, stand up myself or do something to change the physical dynamics.
- He may do the same to male workers. If he does this only to females then it is offensive.

Authors' Interpretation

The hand on the shoulder is touching, yet 52 percent excuse it. He was not fondling or rubbing Ellen's shoulder. Even so, over one-third were annoyed and would discuss it with him. The fact that 23 percent selected "used to it" indicates that this type of behavior may be more pervasive than perhaps is thought. An "innocent" touch? Certainly not considered intimidating by most of the women, this is still inappropriate. Attendees at sexual harassment workshops will learn that this is improper for either male or female. Yet, some individuals of either gender will do so without malice of forethought. The offended party can simply remove the hand and continue in a business-like manner. It is possible to change behavior inoffensively.

SCENARIO 31

As the only woman sales associate in her company, Ellen broke all records for newcomers. She was invited to the company's annual dinner and presented with an award. Each sales associate was called to the podium and thanked by the president. Words bestowed on the men were, "terrific job," "wonderful results," "thanks for your solid contribution." Remarks the first year were not directed to Ellen, but to the crowd in attendance: "What a surprise! I just can't believe how this woman can do this! Can you?" as he handed her the award. After doubling her sales the second year and facing the same award celebration, remarks to the men had not changed. Remarks to the crowd about Ellen had changed only slightly, "She never ceases to amaze me!"

The Women Respond

Women Offended: 70%   **Degree of Offensiveness: 5.3/10**

Predominant Feelings Expressed: **Actions Advised:**
31% Annoyed   43% Discuss with individual
25% Frustrated   19% Ignore

- Hard to choose between "ignore" and "approach president." It doesn't seem to be limiting my salary or recognition or advancement so it may not be worth raising the issue—depending on the attitude of the rest of the company.
- I would explain to him nicely that my results had nothing to do with my gender and that I would appreciate it if he did not mention my gender when talking or praising me.
- Ask him why he doesn't recognize your efforts to be the same as your male counterparts?
- I'd probably look for another firm to work for because what's frightening is that this jackass is truly amazed.
- Explain that you do not like to be singled out—but treated the same as others in the same position.

Authors' Interpretation

Although the company president's intentions might have been noble, his complimentary comments to Ellen are not viewed that way by 70 percent of the women surveyed. Many women will speak to him about it. The message no doubt will be: "Talk to me just like you do to the men!"

This is a classic case of a manager who sees his behavior as giving a reward and the recipient sees it as a punishment. Patronizing a woman is never a rewarding experience. Women do not want *special* treatment, they want *equal* treatment.

SCENARIO 32

Ellen accepted a position as a regional manager for a firm selling services. She reported to a male manager out of town. From the outset he gave far less attention to her business needs than he did to those of her male peers in other cities. After six months, she asked for a meeting to resolve this. One day he called to announce that he was coming to town and would like to take her to dinner, but he had to meet with Mr. X who was "so very important." He told her he would meet her about 9:30 P.M. or 10:00 P.M. After eating a sandwich at her desk at 7:30 P.M., the phone rang. Her manager stated that the dinner had fallen through and she was to have dinner with him at 9:00 P.M. During dinner, no mention was made of business in spite of her efforts. The conversation was personal and included dancing at his insistence. When the restaurant closed at 11:30 P.M., he gripped her arm and moved her to a neighboring bar when she attempted to hail a taxi. At 2:00 A.M., when the bar closed, she hailed a taxi in front. Instead of saying good night, he commented on her "inept performance" in front of bystanders.

The Women Respond

Women Offended: 97%   **Degree of Offensiveness: 8.0/10**

Predominant Feelings Expressed:	**Actions Advised:**
66% Anger	75% Discuss with management
31% Frustrated	25% Discuss with individual
	15% Take legal action
	10% Quit

- Ellen is a fool for letting it go that far. I would never have agreed to a late dinner meeting or even an off-site meeting for a discussion of that nature. Ellen offends me here. I would have documented it with a memo to file.
- His behavior as a manager is uncalled for.
- Document and discuss with higher management.
- She should have left earlier.
- Immediately ask for a meeting in his office to redefine her role as a *professional*. If no results, go to the next level of management. File a complaint as the last resort.

SCENARIO 32 (continued)
Authors' Interpretation

It might be easy to dismiss this offensive scene with the comment that Ellen should have refused to meet her boss. Yet late evening dinner meetings between male employees and male managers are common, especially when the manager is based in another city. The behavior of the out-of-town manager would be just as offensive to a male subordinate who wants and needs to discuss the job and his performance. Few male subordinates would have felt the desire for camaraderie at a bar. Neither a woman nor a man would have found a comfortable way to cut short this evening. They already faced a significant challenge in trying to build a working relationship with an insensitive manager.

Women who wish to move upward in corporations must avail themselves of opportunities to meet informally with management. Proper professional etiquette for these situations is in the embryonic stage. However, the goal must be that no one emerges a loser. Both men and women must focus on building mixed-gender working relationships that enhance productivity and the quality of all of our lives.

SCENARIO 33

Ellen worked in the marketing department of a multinational corporation, reporting to a male supervisor. On many occasions, he made it clear to her that he did not believe women should work full-time. One day he called her to his office to "review some documents from Europe." When she entered, she found a male co-worker sitting across from her boss. Holding out to Ellen a fold-out sample of the advertising, her boss said, "Tell me what you think of this." Then he unveiled the paper. Ellen faced a pin-up poster of a woman wearing only a hat.

The Women Respond

Women Offended: 92%   **Degree of Offensiveness: 7.0/10**

Predominant Feelings Expressed: **Actions Advised:**
44% Angry   51% Discuss with individual
35% Degraded   43% Discuss with management
                                   12% Take legal action

- Another work experience of a woman. The photo perhaps had some value as a marketing concept but one male's mentality was to use it to degrade a co-worker. Repeated offenses should be recorded and reported to management.
- I would take the poster to the marketing department head and say, 'Let's ask her/him what *they* think.' Where's the co-worker respect?
- The male supervisor should learn that women in the workforce are here to stay before it affects his performance.
- If upper management condones such behavior, you're in the wrong company . . . literally.
- Handle the advertising professionally; ask what it is for . . . .

Authors' Interpretation

What will upper management do when 43 percent of the women protest? Will they giggle, laugh or mildly scold the offender, asking him to be more discreet? Or, will they take the time to understand, respect and respond to the women who have been harassed?. This is clearly inappropriate behavior by the manager who thought he was being cute or funny. He must hear a message that his humor *will* change.

SCENARIO 34

As the stock clerk in an auto parts store, Ellen found herself working for a man with a lewd vocabulary and a penchant for unnecessarily putting himself physically close to her. At first he would scratch her back, pull her bra strap, rub his arms next to hers and try to run into her. Deciding she had had enough, she told the owner of the firm, who then spoke to the man. After that, the behavior intensified with closer contact more often. He began to withhold her paycheck until she did him some favor, always requiring "touching," such as scratching his back. In addition, he withheld slips on withdrawals from stock toward the end of the day so that she could never get out of work on time.

The Women Respond

Women Offended: 100%	**Degree of Offensiveness: 9.2/10**

Predominant Feelings Expressed:	**Actions Advised:**
71% Angry	67% Take legal action
28% Degraded	41% Discuss with management
20% Frustrated	28% Quit job

- Outrageous!
- She needs to be more assertive. Scratching one's back to obtain one's check is hard to fathom.
- I would file suit and contact several outside agencies for support.
- He's worse than the one in #12 (electrician supervisor who fondled breasts on ladder); he's infringing on Ellen's time, as well as, person.
- Get this guy fired!

Authors' Interpretation

Management beware! Ellen has spoken with management to no avail. Some will try again, but most will seek legal advice or action to resolve. The comments show very strong reaction. When women go outside the company in these instances, they normally win. Why? Management's response to these complaints is often inaction. They hesitate to reprimand or remove a "key player;" ie, a senior vice president or someone who brings definable income to the bottom line. Regardless of how well a harasser performs his or her job, or at what level, the cost of a legal suit and fines more than eat up any profits they bring in. Angry and degraded, women want action—not excuses.

SCENARIO 35

Ellen's favorite perfume pervaded the office every day. Just as often, one of her male co-workers would walk up close to her while she was at her desk, smell her neck and say, "Oh, your perfume smells so good!"

The Women Respond

Women Offended: 53%   **Degree of Offensiveness: 4.4/10**

Predominant Feelings Expressed: **Actions Advised:**
43% Annoyed   39% Discuss with individual
19% Used to it   11% Ignore

- If he just told her the perfume smelled good it would not be too bad; he doesn't have to smell her neck.
- Would a male go up to another male and do the same if he liked the cologne or after-shave?
- I'd better excuse myself from answering this because I find strong perfume so offensive that I'd approve of almost any behavior that would cause the wearer to discontinue wearing it.
- Perhaps Ellen should apply her perfume a little more judiciously.
- I hate loud perfume and think it's inappropriate in an office, but would expect people to keep their distance from me.

Authors' Interpretation

While offensiveness ran over 50 percent, most women did not defend their right to wear perfume. Collectively, most women who commented stated either "Wear less perfume" or "she's getting what she's asking for." The solution is not difficult to find.

Just as women must dress appropriately, they must choose appropriate "accessories." Throughout history, women have used perfume specifically to attract men. As women rethink their wishes for professional rather than personal/social relationships in the workplace, they might rethink the role of perfume. As one woman responded, "If it pervades the office, it's overdone." On the other hand, both genders must learn to respect each other's "territory." This is definitely an invasion of both territories.

SCENARIO 36

At a college faculty gathering in front of several women full professors, a male junior professor proceeded to share one of the crudest, most vulgar jokes imaginable regarding purposes for a woman's vagina, which he referred to more crudely, and added sadistic comments about dismemberment.

The Women Respond

Women Offended: 96%   **Degree of Offensiveness: 8.2/10**

Predominant Feelings Expressed: **Actions Advised:**
56% Angry   44% Discuss with individual
40% Degraded   42% Discuss with management
 5% Used to it   15% Ignore
                                        12% Take legal action

- Some faculty confuse disgusting behavior with academic freedom.
- I would assume/hope that a group of "intelligent" people would put this guy in his place and would question his accessibility to young students as well.
- In the academic community, such archaic attitudes cannot be tolerated. There are enough witnesses here to get him removed from the tenure track.
- Full professors should write up disciplinary actions on him.
- The junior professor is making a fool of himself.

Authors' Interpretation

The fact that an allegedly educated man is so crude causes an almost unanimous response of highly offensive. Only 15 percent would ignore this incident. Most would work to ensure prevention of his earning tenure or his removal. However, 12 percent would seek agency or legal action. Women who hear these remarks must speak up. Males populate the top of the hierarchy at most universities; rarely do they publicly censure other academics, even those junior to them. Many academics have become accustomed to total freedom within their classrooms. Offenses such as these *must* be curbed.

Blatant sexist behavior cannot be defended, but policies and practices followed as complaints surface will protect management from EEOC or legal suits. Academic environments are workplaces; even students are protected by the law. Workshops to provide sensitivity to faculty as well as administrative employees are definitely in order.

SCENARIO 37

Ellen, a first-year employee and entry-level manager in a large, conservative company, was looking forward to her performance appraisal to see how she could improve her work. She had discussed appraisals with one of her male peers who had received some solid work performance suggestions and mentoring as their boss suggested meetings he should attend and people he should get to know. When Ellen received her verbal appraisal, her manager suggested that she had a "few problems. Her lifestyle was too high, she travelled to too many nice places, she dressed too well, she drove too nice a car." When Ellen asked what these had to do with performance, he volunteered that they "affected perceptions that she would have to change if she wanted to get along there." When she asked again for specific suggestions that would improve her work, she was told to "concentrate on these and bring them under control."

The Women Respond

Women Offended: 92%   **Degree of Offensiveness: 6.9/10**

Predominant Feelings Expressed: **Actions Advised:**
50% Frustrated   58% Discuss with management
46% Angry   25% Discuss with peers
                                                             15% Take legal action
                                                             10% Quit job

- Speaking of perceptions, I hope this manager isn't responsible for company growth. Conservative company or not, if Ellen kept within his work budget, her personal budget should have no bearing on her performance. I would look for an up-to-date company.
- If this had an effect on my career and promotability, I'd immediately take it to higher management. A "high personal lifestyle" is none of their concern.
- I would like to see him commit that to writing before I accept it.
- Tone down—keep personal business out of the office.
- I'd take my "appraisal" to personnel and file a grievance. I cannot help the company if I don't know how to improve.

SCENARIO 37 (continued)

Authors' Interpretation

Gender rather than sexual harassment surfaces here with a very high number of women offended. The percentage rises when the ability to perform one's job is hampered and income is impacted. Twenty-one percent would take serious steps immediately, either legal action or quitting the job. Others advised in the comments that either would be the second step.

A performance appraisal discussion should focus on qualitative and quantitative aspects of performance of the position, hopefully to mutually agreed upon standards. Some discussion of lifestyle perceptions may be positive if those perceptions truly impact negatively on performance. Ellen could have been "flaunting it" and detracting from needed joint productivity/cooperation with her peers. However, since the manager gave no evidence of her lifestyle impacting negatively on her performance, his behavior was patently wrong. Ellen wanted an opportunity to succeed in the company. Women correctly perceived that this would be impossible.

SCENARIO 38

Ellen worked as a welder in a repair shop. Her boss was celebrating his fiftieth birthday and the employees assembled in the center of the room for cake and coffee brought in by the office manager. The office manager also brought the company camera to "record the event." Handing it to one of the welders who volunteered, she proceeded to climb on her boss's lap, cross her legs, lift her skirt up to the top of her legs, and smile into his eyes, as the men whistled, cheered, and cried, "Atta way to go, babe!"

The Women Respond

Women Offended: 82%   **Degree of Offensiveness: 6.1/10**

Predominant Feelings Expressed: **Actions Advised:**
38% Annoyed   29% Ignore
22% Angry   25% Discuss with individual
21% Degraded

- She has no pride and makes other women look bad. I doubt talking to her would help, except to make me look like a prude. I'd put as much distance between us as possible.
- Just slightly offensive; if this woman is comfortable behaving like this, it's her prerogative.
- She deserves to be treated like a piece of trash.
- As long as it's only in fun!
- Oh, help! That's all we need!

Authors' Interpretation

While comments indicate some confusion over who sat on the boss's lap—Ellen or the office manager—the confusion is irrelevant to evaluation of the action. Four out of five women found this scene offensive, yet the comments split decidedly into two groups: the *live and let live* category and the *helplessness/hopelessness* category. While women checked "annoyed" as the most common feeling, the comments showed many would have checked "dismayed" if given that option.

The comments clearly show the dichotomy. Changing the behavior of some men will also require changing the behavior of some women. Why should anyone excuse offensive, sexist behavior just because women are the offenders? As one woman responded, "There is no place at work for such behavior."

SCENARIO 39

Ellen took a job stocking machines for a vending machine company. Most of the machines were in full view of the public. Wanting to succeed, she worked conscientiously, faster than her male counterparts. When everyone gathered early each day for initial assignments, Ellen faced a lot of banter, including lewd jokes and personal remarks about her looks, personal life and motivations. These actions began to escalate until one day she opened a machine in public view and found scrawled inside, "Ellen (last name) sucks the boss's ——." She continued to find the same message every two or three weeks in some machine.

The Women Respond

Women Offended: 99%   **Degree of Offensiveness: 8.3/10**

Predominant Feelings Expressed: **Actions Advised:**
69% Angry   83% Discuss with management
34% Degraded   27% Take legal action
25% Frustrated

- She needs to keep explicit records of her discussions with managers. It sounds like she's on the road to a legitimate EEO complaint.
- Get management to talk to the male workers about this. When management threatens, it is amazing what results can be achieved.
- Some male counterparts are trying to intimidate her to quit, but allow management to find out who it is and fire them to send a message to the other workers.
- *Demand* an apology and immediate removal of the messages. If these were not accomplished post-haste, I would then lodge a formal complaint or suit and quit.
- Tell the manager to find the employee responsible or you will take legal action. This is more than sexual harassment, it is libel and the accuser needs to be held accountable.

Authors' Interpretation

Even though this act did not include physical touching, women perceived it as an attempt to drive Ellen off the job. Women will fight to protect their ability to earn income in the jobs of their choice. Data clearly show their willingness to take action. While 22 percent expressed the choice of legal action as a first step, many others commented that they would follow through with legal action if discussions did not solve the problem.

Grossly offensive, this scenario is also libelous. Management *must* send strong messages to the troops to stop such harassing behaviors. When this type of action occurs, women *will* be taking their cameras on the job.

SCENARIO 40

Ellen was ecstatic. Her manager appointed her to a committee to discuss actions that might be taken regarding assaults on women close to the manufacturing plant where she was employed. The abuse was obvious to the entire city; problems within the geographical area, a poor section of town, were well understood. What was needed, Ellen believed, were solutions and commitment. The most senior manager from her firm who was present was asked his views. He replied that they needed further study to see if their employees were really at risk before committing any company monies. When Ellen was asked her views, she suggested that further study was irrelevant, the problem was acute, and they should go forward. She added, "Being a woman might affect my answer. Men tend not to get raped but women do." The following day Ellen's manager called her into his office and advised her that "perhaps she could find a less strident and less public way to share her views if she wanted to get ahead in the company."

The Women Respond

Women Offended: 80%   **Degree of Offensiveness: 6.3/10**

Predominant Feelings Expressed: **Actions Advised:**
31% Frustrated   42% Discuss with individual
30% Annoyed   29% Discuss with manager
25% Angry

- The company is addressing the problem through a committee, which is a step in the right direction. Ellen should work with the committee to propose a solution that management can agree with.
- Try to explain once again the threat of being a woman that warranted a strong response.
- Go slowly to change people.
- Ellen could have gotten her point across more tactfully—maybe she did go a little overboard. Try another approach and see what happens—maybe it's just a misunderstanding so far.
- Propose solutions with other peers.

Authors' Interpretation

Most women did not see this as a sexual or gender issue, but as a reversal of empowerment. This, coupled with a lack of sensitivity to the issue of attacks on women, led them to determine its level of offensiveness. Comments indicate that most women were concerned first with solving the problem of their security and second with "their rights" in this situation, as selected comments showed.

SCENARIO 40 (continued)

As stated by one of the respondents, "Bosses don't like to be contradicted. A team player should be able to get her point across non-combatively." Even with excellent interpersonal skills, one does not get ahead by disagreeing with a senior member of management in public. Unfortunately, politics has the upper hand in this situation. Empowerment is gaining favor in the workplace. However, empowerment will appear to be a farce if management doesn't give serious suggestions the weight they deserve. In the meantime, management should attempt to understand the very volatile issue of rape and physical assault from the viewpoint of women.

SCENARIO 41

As administrative manager for the engineering department of a major manufacturing firm, Ellen had to prepare the annual budget for the group's 1,000+ personnel. She was also responsible for negotiating changes with individual managers in order to meet the total department budget. For more than three years, one of the engineering managers had continually attempted to make her life miserable by withholding requested information or reports until the last minute. This year was no different. The appointed day for submission came and went. The week set aside for analysis, negotiations and presentation preparation came and went. At 6:00 P.M., the day before the budget review by higher management was scheduled, this engineering manager dropped off the information at her desk, stating, "I'll be home with a martini or two if you have any questions tonight." He added facetiously, "I'll even stay up late if it will help you out."

The Women Respond

Women Offended: 87%   Degree of Offensiveness: 6.7/10

Predominant Feelings Expressed: Actions Advised:
57% Angry   66% Discuss with management
43% Frustrated   32% Discuss with individual

- Intimidate him.
- This is a management issue. This guy is obviously attempting to display his power.
- Do not include his submission and embarrass him to the max. Make it clear that *he* is the problem.
- Anyone infringing on my time . . . .is highly offensive.
- "Propositions" can be ignored. His delay in providing critical business information is offensive and should be escalated.

Authors' Interpretation

These responses confirm that feelings move from annoyance to anger and frustration when actions occur that interfere with job performance. Sexual innuendoes played no part. Yet, a majority would take action. The classic power bully is at work here. He/she attacks women and men. A woman faces more serious repercussions in attacking this problem—many men still question whether women are team players. If she complains, she loses face and risks her image as a team player. Yet, fighting fire with fire; i.e., leaving out the budget, penalizes the company. Power games always impact productivity. If a woman has the support of her manager, her best course of action is to level with him/her, state that she abhors playing games and ask his/her advice on how to proceed.

SCENARIO 42

Ellen finished her first year in college and took a position for the summer as an assistant to a veterinarian at an animal clinic open 24 hours a day. She was assigned the evening shift from 5:00 P.M. to 1:00 A.M. The workload varied, with activity dropping off later in the evening. Often Ellen was alone with the veterinarian on duty for long periods of time. The vet stayed overnight in a bedroom adjacent to the office. One of the three veterinarians who rotated shifts, an older married male, began making comments about nothing to do, which advanced to suggesting that he and Ellen go in the bedroom and "have a quickie." Comments like this became routine. Because of his demeanor, Ellen could never tell if he was serious, if he was waiting for her reaction each day, or if he was only joking.

The Women Respond

Women Offended: 93%   **Degree of Offensiveness: 6.4/10**

Predominant Feelings Expressed: **Actions Advised:**
52% Annoyed   60% Discuss with individual
22% Angry   16% Ignore it
17% Degraded   14% Quit job
16% Intimidated

- I would *definitely* let the other vets and my parents know and have the vets put a stop to it. I would also refuse to work the night shift and refuse to work any further with that particular vet. I'd probably leave that office.
- Confront him—depending on his reaction, she may need to talk to management or EEO.
- Tell him to keep his quickies to himself.
- This guy is testing the water. It's a typical aggressive male technique which should be nipped at the bud or will continue.
- Even if he was kidding, he was still harassing her.

SCENARIO 42 (continued)
Authors' Interpretation

The vet was probably joking, since the contributor of this scenario was never assaulted or talked into the bedroom. But, this is not a joking matter in the minds of 93 percent of the women. With all the talk and acts of date/rape on college campuses, a college-aged woman alone with an older man at this late hour talking about quickies would unsettle even the most confident 19-year-old. Discussions with academia show that young women have more difficulty than older women in dealing with the power of their elders. When an employee complains to a manager (or any veterinarian) about this situation, management must do something about it with no retaliation toward the employee. Further, they might well be advised to move her to a day shift. She could quit, but what a lose-lose situation for a woman earning her way through college.

SCENARIO 43

Ellen joined a small, conservative law firm. As the only woman lawyer, she was treated with solid respect by the senior partner who hired her. He read her briefs and gave her good feedback on her work. The male lawyers on staff, none of whom had wives who worked outside the home, did not overtly comment on her "need for a career" nor speak negatively about her work. However, she continually faced greetings and comments such as, "Hi, Babe." "Atta girl!" "Hon" and "Dear" replaced her first name. Often she overheard comments such as, "What do you mean your wife won't? Tell her, don't ask her!" She lunched with them rarely and only at her instigation.

The Women Respond

Women Offended: 72%   **Degree of Offensiveness: 4.2/10**

Predominant Feelings Expressed: **Actions Advised:**
45% Annoyed   30% Discuss with individuals
29% Used to it   26% Ignore
                                     17% Discuss with management

- She had better get to know her co-workers if she hopes to affect their behavior toward her.
- I probably would mention this to the senior partner off the record.
- The only way to overcome this is to earn their respect one by one. I would ask them to call me by my name.
- I would assume she's too busy with her work to reform and educate the males in the office.
- It would not do any good to make a mountain out of this. They do not judge your work.

Authors' Interpretation

Offended or not, no one would quit. A ray of hope—the senior partner treats Ellen with respect. Comments were split about 50/50, with one group counseling Ellen to work it out and the other counseling her to speak up, either nicely or stridently. While many women will ignore this treatment by peers today as par for the course, it will unlikely be *par* for long as more women speak up rather than ignore (30 percent versus 20 percent) such annoying and demeaning treatment.

Ellen's peers may give her a hard time because she is a woman— a double whammy may be that she is perceived as the high potential, or the fair-haired person. The best strategy for Ellen is to divide and conquer. One by one, she should build rapport from the least offensive to the most offensive person. One by one, ask their advice about a case, etc. Build a respectable working relationship. One may never change the most offensive person, but you will soon have some allies who are enjoyable to be around.

SCENARIO 44

Newly hired as a financial analyst by a manufacturing firm, Ellen was assigned to the marketing department. While several women populated the sales force, Ellen was the only woman in marketing. The marketing team was challenged to come up with a totally new in-house campaign to excite the sales force since sales were sagging in the recessionary economy. Ellen was expected to participate with creative ideas. The first session was free flowing, with many bawdy suggestions and much laughter. When the dust settled, "the team vote" decided the theme: "Let's kick the competition in the balls!" Each week of the 15-week campaign was "round one, round two," etc. Taking away from a competitor an order over $25,000 was billed as a "knockout punch" with a $200 bonus. The prize recommended at contest end for the top five producers was the use of chauffeured limos to ferry winners and spouses back and forth from dinner and the Bulls-Lakers game.

The Women Respond

Women Offended: 53%　　　　　**Degree of Offensiveness: 4.3/10**

Predominant Feelings Expressed:　　**Actions Advised:**
31% Annoyed　　　　　　　　　　23% Ignore
12% Frustrated　　　　　　　　　10% Discuss with management

- Go with it this year. Attempt to change it next opportunity.
- A good marketing team should know their audience. They sound too narrow-minded. Join the '90s.
- Her time to voice her opinion was at the team vote.
- I love sports!
- The company's basic philosophy is dreadful and if shared with consumers—women being primary purchasers of most things—would be disastrous . . . .

Authors' Interpretation

Obviously, it's still a male-dominated workforce . . . .

If you "kick the competition in the balls" in the year 2000, you will bypass too much of the competition to survive. You will insult even more women at higher levels. External competition is healthy. We need fun campaign slogans and excitement to move the team to win. But, can't we channel some of the brainpower of both genders to create a more appropriate slogan?

SCENARIO 45

Most of the technicians in the electronics lab were men when Ellen joined her new firm in a new city. She was well-trained and had just completed a two-year stint working for another firm where she had received high marks for her good work. Ellen found the new atmosphere laid back, the banter lively at break time. Topics varied, but certain employees outside the lab were treated in soap opera fashion with running commentaries. They were given names, such as the "bimbo secretary," the "bitch in personnel who just needs a good lay," the "new knocker out on the floor." Bikini-clad models peppered the walls. When they included a very explicit sexual joke, they would watch Ellen's reaction to see if she understood it or not, and then taunt her one way or the other. When she complained to management, she was told that this was harmless, just the usual male behavior in this type of environment.

The Women Respond

Women Offended: 92%   **Degree of Offensiveness: 6.5/10**

Predominant Feelings Expressed:	Actions Advised:
42% Annoyed	35% Take legal action
38% Angry	23% Discuss with management
26% Degraded	22% Quit job

- I have never complained to management, but this same thing goes on with women. They can be just as bad and in some cases worse than men.
- Usual male "adult" behavior should not include taunts. If they want to be children, they shouldn't require an audience.
- Horrible place to work! Seek new employment immediately.
- As a well-trained, hard worker, Ellen could surely work in a more receptive, progressive environment than this!
- Management must revise the type of environment caused by the "usual male behavior." Since management was confronted to no avail, a formal complaint should be filed.

Authors' Interpretation

This is another case of males trying to keep a woman out of a male-dominated, higher paying job, by creating an uncomfortable, hostile, work environment! Women perceived this correctly—as an attack upon their earning power, with 32 percent electing to take legal action. The 19 percent who would quit would find a job easily because of the lack of workers with this high-tech skill. At this level of offensiveness, few women who commented elected to take their break someplace else.

Once again, management needs to beware! Payment is less for remedial training than lower productivity, attrition, court costs and fees. Your choice.

SCENARIO 46

Ellen, just out of high school, had a job that gave her the opportunity to speak regularly with most of the employees in her building. She soon knew most of them fairly well and felt comfortable with them. During the Christmas season, she attended the "employees only" company party, arriving with three other women. The party lasted until midnight instead of 8 P.M. as planned. When it ended, Ellen and one of the other women realized their friends had left without them and they needed transportation home. Two men from accounting offered them a ride home. The following Monday Ellen asked one of the women why she left without them, stating they had to "bum a ride home with Joe and Bill from accounting." Ellen's boss, who had overheard the comment, called her into his office and said, "I know you're new to the workforce, so I thought I would mention that next time you might want to take a taxi home from a company event rather than going home with married men. I'm sure this was very innocent, but this town is not that big and not everyone else might think the same way I do."

The Women Respond

Women Offended: 47%   **Degree of Offensiveness: 5.1/10**

Predominant Feelings Expressed: **Actions Advised:**
30% Annoyed   22% Discuss with individual
18% Puzzled   16% Ignore

- Offensive that he is exaggerating an innocent circumstance and she is sorry he looks at it like that.
- As a woman you are under more scrutiny and have to be more discreet than a man. This is not fair, but it is true.
- The manager could be saving Ellen from future heartache.
- She was only getting a ride home!
- Let him know that it was harmless and thank him for the tip.

Authors' Interpretation

A tough one! Our culture tends to support the tip given by Ellen's boss. But this same culture fosters and preserves the discrimination of women's work and men's work. We must be able to have men and women work and socialize together as they do within the same gender. The high level of offensiveness here surprised the authors. Most women believed the man was trying to be helpful. However, some believe he inferred that Ellen and her friend acted inappropriately. Women can learn from this, however, that what appears to be innocent may cause the wrong impression.

SCENARIO 47

While Ellen was a cocktail waitress at a resort hotel bar, she often faced rowdy groups of conference attendees. Occasionally, as she bent over to serve their drinks, one of the men would pat her on the fanny, with or without additional comments about her anatomy. She complained to management, who informed her that the situation was beyond their ability to control. The occasional pats continued, depending upon the type of crowd in attendance.

The Women Respond

Women Offended: 82%   **Degree of Offensiveness: 7.0/10**

Predominant Feelings Expressed: **Actions Advised:**
36% Annoyed   60% Quit job
36% Angry   17% Take legal action
24% Degraded   13% Discuss with individuals

- A male waiter might get the same response from women (or men). This type of position probably gets these responses.
- Management can control the situation and should do so!
- No matter how hard management tries, it will probably continue.
- Goes with the job from what I hear.
- The worst Catch 22—yell at the offending customers and get no tips; management says it's beyond control; the women need the money. Maybe I'd try and ignore it and look for another job.

Authors' Interpretation

In this second scenario involving a waitress and "pats on the fanny," the offenders are customers and not the boss. Just as in Scenario eight, most would quit the job, but fewer would seek legal action. Why is it that in occupations such as waitress and flight attendant, women must face customers who believe they have open season for sexual remarks and careless hands? Where is respect? Should over one and one-half million women in these occupations be forced to accept offensive behavior as a condition of employment? Men view these women in a "social setting" that includes sex, rather than as women in their working environment. While some women might bring on some of this behavior, it's safe to say that one and one-half million don't!!! Please!!

Can an owner stay in business by getting tough on customers who are offensive? A pragmatist would say no. The law says they must attempt to control the environment. In the meantime, women might be well advised to help by following the advice of one respondent, "I'd just smile, remove their hands, and tell them my 6'7" boyfriend wouldn't like them to do that again!" Sexist? Yes! Will it work? Probably! Wish there were a better answer!

SCENARIO 48

Ellen accepted a position on the night shift at a food manufacturing plant. Whenever she took her break from her position folding cartons to fill with bottles of sauce coming down the assembly line, she was followed into the break room by her foreman. He would fix her a cup of coffee, hand it to her and as often as possible angle her into the corner of the room where he proceeded to give her running details of his non-existent sex life at home. Compliments about her looks would follow, possibly as an attempt to soften her for the request, which was always "when are you going to agree to meet me in my van in the parking lot during the break and help me out. You know if you help me I can help you. I can get you promoted to a supervisor with the right motivation."

The Women Respond

Women Offended: 100%   **Degree of Offensiveness: 8.8/10**

Predominant Feelings Expressed: **Actions Advised:**
79% Angry   73% Discuss with management
26% Degraded   36% Discuss with individual
                                              32% Take legal action

- . . . get co-workers to verify his behavior and take breaks with you.
- Needs to be fired or action will be taken with EEO.
- Why allow this in the first place?
- I'd call his wife and suggest they both seriously consider marriage counseling or sex therapy and tell her what was going on.
- He'd wear the coffee!

Authors' Interpretation

Finally, a clear case of *quid pro quo*, or asking for sexual favors in exchange for favoritism on the job. As shown before, women will fight to retain their jobs and provide for their economic livelihood. As data reflect here, degrading a woman only compounds the situation and raises the level of offensiveness.

After one incident such as this, the harassed should take immediate action. We suggest that Ellen talk not just to the harasser but to others. Go first to management. If it is not resolved immediately, visit a lawyer or EEOC. Management must open their eyes and ears to this harassing behavior and shut it down. A well conceived attitude survey is an inexpensive and effective tool to assess the climate. This also tells your employees of your seriousness regarding harassment and discrimination.

SCENARIO 49

As a new sales associate for a manufacturing firm, Ellen interviewed with her potential boss who was cordial. He told Ellen how impressed he was with her credentials and her potential with the company. When he offered her the position, he stated that she had been selected from a very large pool of highly qualified candidates. Naturally, she was excited. Her boss initially gave her some "easy sales," and referred to her as "the rookie." He told her he would continue to handle the "tough stuff." When Ellen went to him to obtain further information about an account, he would often take it away from her, saying, "You can't go there. That guy will take advantage of you. I'll have to handle this." When he introduced her to clients, he still called her "the rookie." She was never invited to lunch with a client or on joint calls; when he returned he would tell Ellen he had "resolved all the problems and struck a deal." Her boss "neglected" to tell her about a sales seminar. When she confronted him, he stated, "You can't go at this time, but you wouldn't like it anyway—all the guys would be hitting on you." Ellen realized that her career was going to suffer and spoke to him about it, telling him she wanted fair treatment; he ignored this. When his boss asked him how Ellen was coming along, he stated, "She may make it, but I'm not sure. It's tough. I can't send her on the road alone. Most of our customers won't deal with a woman."

The Women Respond

Women Offended: 95%   **Degree of Offensiveness: 8.0/10**

Predominant Feelings Expressed:	Actions Advised:
62% Angry	79% Discuss with management
48% Frustration	27% Discuss with individual
	14% Quit job
	15% Take legal action

- This could happen to a male who is new to the department. You have to demonstrate ability and apparently she hasn't.
- Ellen's boss is affecting her performance and possibly her career in the firm with old-fashioned behavior and snake-in-the-grass words.
- He is the one who doesn't want to deal with a woman . . . .
- The frustration is from never being given an opportunity to try.
- I think this is a real situation and hard to define. *We* have to stay on the ball as far as comments made to keep an employee from being second rated. It's tough. You almost have to record conversations and PREPARE YOURSELF!

SCENARIO 49 (continued)
Authors' Interpretation

Data show strong reaction to gender harassment that precludes women from doing their jobs. One out of 10 would turn quickly to EEOC or take legal action. Managements must realize that some managers merely comply with a company's affirmative action plan. They meet the hiring goal and the letter of the law, but they never meet the spirit of the law. They routinely exclude top performers from functioning in their jobs, especially women and minorities. In the 1970s, many managements increased the number of women in exempt level jobs—by changing titles and pay rates. Still the women performed the work of clerks. If this mentality continues, it will be impossible to attract and retain the qualified women needed in the workforce of the future. Take a careful look at the number of women graduates of key MBA schools and see how few stay with Fortune 500 companies.

SCENARIO 50

Ellen, a senior manager in her firm, had worked late into the night on her presentation for her manager's staff meeting. She wanted to ensure that the material was accurate and her presentation smooth. As she entered the meeting the next morning, she was followed by a peer who whispered audibly to her, in the presence of others, "What color are you wearing underneath today, Ellen?"

The Women Respond

Women Offended: 96%   Degree of Offensiveness: 7.3/10

Predominant Feelings Expressed: **Actions Advised:**
53% Angry   64% Discuss with individual
41% Annoyed   23% Discuss with management
23% Degraded   3% Take legal action

- Guaranteed I would have trouble keeping my thoughts clear after that—too personal.
- In a manager's presence, I would loudly ask, "Excuse me? What did you just ask me? Are you always such a professional fool?" Go on with meeting. I would definitely follow up with a complaint.
- Ignore this. Show them you can handle it despite the pressure.
- Comment should not be dignified. Later, discuss with the individual to determine his (?) motivation and goal in making the statement.
- Smack him and ask him what business it is of his.

Authors' Interpretation

Male-dominated environments include senior levels of management. Physical attacks are rare, replaced by psychological attacks. Those men who continue to harass should expect more physical and verbal counterattacks. This survey clearly shows that women realize it is now okay to show anger. When they also realize that they must show anger to cleanse themselves before they can "get on with their presentation," they will. Few women could remain calm and concentrate in the face of such a demeaning statement—obviously the intent of the harasser. Expect more anger. It's healthier and more productive.

Chapter Two

The Impact of Social and Legal Changes

SOCIAL CHANGE IN THE TWENTIETH CENTURY

Before the decade of the '90s closes, far more American women and men will have forged new relationships both personally and professionally. Ideas—and the needs of women—have changed.

Technology has changed radically the way we work—brains increasingly count for more than brawn in most U.S. workplaces. In the past, most women couldn't scale telephone poles or carry the equipment needed for line repairs. Today, equipment is far lighter and more often than not a call to a central computer will restore or change telephone service. The interpersonal skills needed to deal with irate customers have become more important than manual skills. In a majority of jobs, "heavy work" is no longer "heavy work." In most job classifications, women are now as advantaged as men in meeting job requirements and performing work.

The law has responded to provide women with more opportunity. While changing laws is difficult, changing mindsets is an even greater challenge. Although laws changed in the 1960s, the movement to end job segregation *crawled* during the '70s and the '80s. In the '90s, however, two important trends provide women with the impetus to change this. First, social interaction between women and men is changing. Second, women today see themselves as lifelong participants in the workforce, rather than homemakers, aware of their rights and their potential gains. Women and the law alone, however, are not enough to make significant inroads. Business and academia must work together to help shape a future that fully utilizes the talents of every member of society.

Prior to the *Equal Pay Act of 1963* and *Title VII of the Civil Rights Act of 1964*, work was defined as either *light* (women's work) or *heavy*, (men's work.) State laws often restricted the number of hours per day, days per week and pounds of lifting that women could perform legally. Obviously, *heavy work* paid more than *light work*. Not even women questioned why they could move 200 pound patients in, out or around hospital beds to treat or wash them, or move rooms of furniture, often including pianos, to vacuum under and behind them, but could not perform *heavy work* in the workplace. That simply was "the way it was."

Begun in the late '60s, the feminist movement focused on personal as well as job-related issues, setting in motion changes in social mores. Women and men walked picket lines side by side. Far more women entered college, professional schools and the workplace in jobs equal to those of men. Education at all levels began to include both team and individual orientations. As women and men learned and worked together toward common goals, they began to develop friendships and working relationships previously frowned upon.

"... a real career-oriented person does not want to be an office adornment whether male or female."

The ancient Greek philosopher Plato argued that women and men could form what we now call "Platonic friendships,"—friendships between members of the opposite sex not based upon sexual attraction. Two thousand five hundred years later, that theory is now being tested in our workplaces.

Women and men are facing changing social mores *now*. Women increasingly realize that they need not take abuse and/or discrimination—in personal relationships, access to money or the ability to function effectively in the workforce in positions of their choice. They are divorcing abusive husbands and, if necessary, moving into shelters. They are filing charges against employers for pay disparity and harassment.

Women and the legal community have led this social change. While no new law was created between 1964 and 1991, individual judges who have come face-to-face with outrageous harassing and discriminatory behavior in their courtrooms have handed down landmark decisions. Often the behaviors in question were ignored by business and academia. Laws exist to keep predators from devouring those less able to defend themselves. Women and minorities fall into that category by virtue of limited access to power, not less talent. Women, minorities and courtrooms will continue to insist upon fair treatment and respect in the workplace. The sheer numbers of women lodging formal complaints, either to employers or outside agencies, will continue to swell and surround women, giving them greater protection from the fear of retaliation or professional suicide.

"If I'm in the same job, I'm their equal."

To remain competitive in an increasingly international world, employers need all the talent they can muster. Those who do not understand the advantage of using the talents of their entire workforce will be forced to take notice. Women and minorities will continue to provide the expansion of the workforce—81 percent of all marriages will be dual career by 1995. Harassment and discrimination will be viewed as negatives to profitability, robbing employers of needed talent and consuming profits when dollars are spent on lawsuits and/or out-of-court settlements. Adherence to the law will become a primary driver of social change, for practical, if not moral reasons. It behooves employers to closely examine the law.

HOW THE LAW HAS DEVELOPED

Prior to 1963, no laws dealt with discrimination. Employees were not protected under common law. In fact, common law considered the employment relationship to be a private contractual matter in which judicial interference played no part.

Since 1963, however, the United States legislature has concerned itself with providing equal opportunity to individuals regardless of accidents of nature or personal beliefs. Most current law is embodied in the *Equal Pay Act of 1963* and *Title VII of the 1964 Civil Rights Act*. This legislation provided protection against discrimination and disparate treatment to everyone, regardless of race, religion, color, sex or national origin. Workers over the age of 40, the handicapped and pregnant employees were incorporated into the law as protected classes as part of *Title VII* in 1967, 1973 and 1975 respectively. In 1972, the Equal Employment Opportunity Commission (EEOC) was established to enforce *Title VII of the 1964 Civil Right Act*.

Within this basic framework, the law has been refined primarily through three avenues: in the courts in landmark cases, in updated guidelines from the EEOC and in further legislation in 1991. While sexual harassment was covered as a sub-topic under *Title VII of the 1964 Civil Rights Act*, it achieved a life of its own when its importance as a workplace irritant to women began to escalate. This offense clearly has been shaped by court cases since the mid-1980s.

During 1991, significant changes occurred to stop sexual harassment and prosecute offenders. The EEOC announced that it had removed sexual harassment claims from the mainstream of job discrimination claims and would speed up claim processing. When necessary, employers will be ordered by the federal courts to cease the alleged behavior while claims are under investigation.

"In a working environment, there is no such thing as a 'harmless remark.' There needs to be a change in this type of management thinking."

As mentioned in Chapter 1, the U.S. Appeals Court for the Ninth Circuit used a new standard in 1991 to define a hostile work environment, mandating that the facts in such cases be viewed from the perspective of a "reasonable woman," not a reasonable man, when the harassee is female. The determinant is the perspective of the *victim*, not the perpetrator of the offense.

Contemporaneous to these events was the development of a new body of law passed by the U.S. House and the U.S. Senate late last year as the *1991 Civil Rights Bill*. The new law makes it far easier to file and win sex discrimination suits against employers who intentionally discriminate. Some employers believe that the law *implies* the use of quotas to avoid charges of disparate treatment with respect to hiring and promoting women and minorities, since it shifts the burden of proof of unintentional discrimination back to employers.

"Doesn't top management ever get involved with the behavior of their managers?"

The new law caps compensatory and punitive awards based upon company size and clearly states that punitive damage awards apply only to *intentional* discrimination that causes disparate impact. Sexual harassment as part of sex discrimination can be viewed as intentional and is now subject to punitive damage awards. Thus, much larger sums of money can be won by victims of all forms of discrimination, including sex and sexual harassment, with favorable court rulings. The new law applies to hiring, on-the-job problems such as promotion and harassment, and dismissal.

Prior to 1991, sexual harassment cases were filed only by individuals. The final act of 1991 that substantially furthered the ability of sexual harassment victims to take advantage of the law, was the resolution of a court case in Minneapolis. There, a federal judge ruled that class action suits for sexual harassment were valid when large groups of women claim that hostility is pervasive in their work environment. This certainly will help women enter previously male-dominated environments and open areas of work that have been non-traditionally female.

The floodgates have opened. Women will still need encouragement, however, to exercise their legal options. It is hoped that a broader understanding of the law by all parties concerned will lower significantly the incidence of harassment and its legal ramifications.

CURRENT SEXUAL HARASSMENT LAWS: DEFINED AND EXPLAINED

Current sexual harassment law under EEOC guidelines on discrimination because of sex, codified at 29 C.F.R., §1604.11 states the following:

§1604.11 *Sexual Harassment.*

(a) Harassment on the basis of sex is a violation of section 703 of Title VII.[1] Unwelcome sexual advances, requests for sexual favors, and other verbal or physical conduct of a sexual nature constitute sexual harassment when (1) submission to such conduct is made either explicitly or implicitly a term or condition of an individual's employment, (2) submission to or rejection of such conduct by an individual is used as the basis for employment decisions affecting such individual, or (3) such conduct has the purpose or effect of unreasonably interfering with an individual's work performance or creating an intimidating, hostile, or offensive working environment.

(b) In determining whether alleged conduct constitutes sexual harassment, the Commission will look at the record as a whole and at the totality of the

---

[1]The principles involved here continue to apply to race, color, religion or national origin.

circumstances, such as the nature of the sexual advances and the context in which the alleged incidents occurred. The determination of the legality of a particular action will be made from the facts, on a case by case basis.

(c) Applying general Title VII principles, an employer, employment agency, joint apprenticeship committee or labor organization (hereinafter collectively referred to as "employer") is responsible for its acts and those of its agents and supervisory employees with respect to sexual harassment regardless of whether the specific acts complained of were authorized or even forbidden by the employer and regardless of whether the employer knew or should have known of their occurrence. The Commission will examine the circumstances of the particular employment relationship and the job functions performed by the individual in determining whether an individual acts in either a supervisory or agency capacity.

(d) With respect to conduct between fellow employees, an employer is responsible for acts of sexual harassment in the workplace where the employer (or its agents or supervisory employees) knows or should have known of the conduct, unless it can show that it took immediate and appropriate corrective action.

(e) An employer may also be responsible for the acts of non-employees, with respect to sexual harassment of employees in the workplace, where the employer (or its agents or supervisory employees) knows or should have known of the conduct and fails to take immediate and appropriate corrective action. In reviewing these cases the Commission will consider the extent of the employer's control and any other legal responsibility which the employer may have with respect to the conduct of such non-employees.

(f) Prevention is the best tool for the elimination of sexual harassment. An employer should take all steps necessary to prevent sexual harassment from occurring, such as affirmatively raising the subject, expressing strong disapproval, developing appropriate sanctions, informing employees of their right to raise and how to raise the issue of harassment under Title VII, and developing methods to sensitize all concerned.

(g) Other related practices: Where employment opportunities or benefits are granted because of an individual's submission to the employer's sexual advances or requests for sexual favors, the employer may be held liable for unlawful sex discrimination against other persons who were qualified for but denied that employment opportunity or benefit.

An Interpretation

Commissioner Joyce Tucker, EEOC, addressed clients of the Chicago law firm of Winston & Strawn in December, 1991, at which time she defined terms, highlighted the important conditions of the law and shared EEOC's current interpretation, as follows:

Sex Harassment versus Sexual Harassment . . . Sex harassment is harassment because of gender, but not harassment of a sexual nature. This can be abusive, rude or intimidating behavior. Sexual harassment is treatment of a sexual nature when submission is made a condition of employment, used as a basis for employment decisions or affects work through the creation of a hostile work environment. Both types of behavior constitute sex discrimination.

Unwelcome . . . For an action to be considered harassment, it must be unwelcome by the individual toward whom it is directed. Commissioner Tucker stated that a key component in the determination of harassment is whether or not the victim told the aggressor or conducted herself/himself to communicate specifically that this conduct is/was unwelcome. If a victim acts as a sexual aggressor and commonly, not occasionally, uses sexual language particularly with the harasser, she/he will have difficulty showing that sexual requests and innuendos are unwelcome, since "the Commission will look at the record as a whole and at the totality of the circumstances and the context in which the alleged incidents occurred."

Quid pro quo . . . This Latin term, literally "this for that," provides a label for behavior by supervisors or members of management who request sexual favors in return for favoritism in employment. The law states that unwelcome sexual conduct violates *Title VII*:

> when (1) submission to such conduct is made either explicitly or implicitly a term or condition of an individual's employment, or (2) submission to or rejection of such conduct by an individual is used as the basis for employment decisions affecting such individual.

Hostile Work Environment . . . This term is used to cover work environments that allow specific behaviors when:

> (3) such conduct has the purpose or effect of unreasonably interfering with an individual's work performance or creating an intimidating, hostile or offensive working environment.

Commissioner Tucker further explained that to create a hostile work environment, behavior would have to be sufficiently severe and pervasive. Language such as *dear*, or *baby*, while annoying, probably would not establish a hostile environment. However, repeated subjection to language or visuals referring to body parts would constitute such an environment.

An employer is liable for *hostile environment by a supervisor*, despite the lack of actual or constructive knowledge, if that employer failed to adopt an explicit policy against sexual harassment and an effective grievance procedure. Contrast this with *quid pro quo* where an employer is always liable regardless of lack of knowledge. In the same context, employers are also responsible for others acting for them; i.e., employment agencies, joint apprenticeship committees or labor organizations.

Peers . . . Employers are responsible for conduct between fellow employees when they actually know or should have known of the conduct, unless they took immediate, decisive, corrective action sufficient to stop the behavior. Firing is not necessary. Removal of the victim from the job or work site—rather than removal of the harasser—is not allowed to accomplish the goal of stopping the behavior.

Non-employees . . . Employers are further responsible for the conduct of "visitors" to their work sites. Vendors, customers, clients and other third parties fall into this category. Employer responsibility is determined by their knowledge of offensive behavior and their degree of control. For example, an office machine service person who regularly attempts to fondle women would be far more within the control of management than are customers of a bar or restaurant.

Commissioner Tucker shared that one *quid pro quo* action would probably constitute harassment, while a hostile work environment charge would be determined by the level and pattern of activity. The more severe the conduct, the less need there is to show quantity and/or pattern, especially when the actions are physical rather than verbal. EEOC currently presumes that unwelcome touching, especially of private body parts, is sufficient to create a hostile environment. Further, if the hostile work environment results in constructive discharge (when an employee believes it is necessary to quit her/his job), the offensive actions would constitute a *quid pro quo*. Employers must guarantee a workplace that will not force employees to quit.

Rules of Evidence

Rules of evidence are not the same in an agency as in a court of law. EEOC will deal with hearsay to determine the credibility of both parties involved. The agency will act only upon charges of events that are both unwelcome and contemporaneous, or filed in a timely manner. Unfortunately, most harassment occurs unseen— in private—and a determination of whether *Title VII* has been violated depends upon the credibility/conduct of individuals.

The victim's account must be sufficiently detailed and credible The harasser's story will carry little weight if other women surface the same complaints. The obligation to speak up to both harassers and employers with accounts of unwanted attention or discrimination is placed *directly upon the victims*. This is for their immediate benefit but also for the benefit of other women who may be experiencing similar problems.

Sexual activity alone does not violate the law. *Title VII* does not prohibit consensual relationships. However, if a person has engaged in voluntary sexual activity with an individual and then changed her/his mind, clearly tells that individual that his/her attention is no longer welcome, and tells her/his employer, harassment can be charged for subsequent conduct by that individual.

Escalating Charges

Discrimination exists in all workplaces. Unions were formed and seniority systems established in an attempt to prevent favoritism. Not all types of favoritism violate the law. Women may consider an action harassment, but if it equally disadvantages men, the conduct is not necessarily actionable. If, however, the favoritism is based upon coercion, it is actionable. In the same vein, bisexual harassment does not necessarily violate the sex discrimination law. Even *quid pro quo* harassment might not be actionable if it is undertaken by a supervisor against women and men. Since laws vary from state to state, employers are urged to review state as well as federal laws governing harassment and discrimination.

With the influx of 1991 legislation and court rulings, and the media explosion of the topic of sexual harassment, charges are escalating. Understanding *how* sexual harassment plays out in the workplace and *why* discriminatory actions happen is key to changing behavior and is more necessary now than ever before.

> *". . . if it's a workplace, then keep it a workplace for everyone."*

Chapter Three

The Workplace Today

THE WORKPLACE TODAY: IN TRANSITION

No one really knows if sexual harassment is more prevalent in the workplace today than it was 10, 20 or 30 years ago. One thing's for certain—it is more visible. The roles of individuals in the workplace change the balance of both opportunity and power through mixed-gender peer teamwork, combined travel and entertainment and the promotion of women into managerial positions. In the past, most victims did not speak up even to friends or peers about the sexual advances or suggestive remarks made to them. Often women were embarrassed, believing as many victims do that they were somehow at fault, that sexual innuendos and requests should not be directed at "nice girls." Anger and resentment against harassing behaviors are now more vocal.

Bringing sexual harassment out in the open makes evident specific behavior patterns. Eighty-five to ninety-five percent of reported harassment appears to be directed toward women, and women are now speaking to co-workers and/or employers or filing charges to counteract this. The extent of harassment of males by females is not known. Men tend not to share their "inability to take care of themselves." But, reverse harassment is evident. Some women practice reactive sexual harassment and annoy male peers in an attempt to stop unwelcome male behavior.

Women Today

Many women today are more gender liberated. Taking a proactive stance, they meet with mixed reactions, and send mixed signals to men. Single women now ask men for dates, seeing the workplace as a good place to shop for romance and social life. Often they try to walk a fine line between being sexy, letting individuals know they are available, and wishing to be respectable and *feminine*. It's a tough act. Some succeed; others do not. Women have always viewed the workplace more as a social setting than have men. Further complicating the problem, women today have joined the fitness craze and honed their bodies to perfection. Women and clothing designers have decided to show off as much as possible. The liberating behaviors of today simply complicate the issue of sex harassment.

> *"Women FREQUENTLY invite harassment. It is not at all unusual for a group of women to revel in ribald humor. I completely understand men's confusion—I'm quite confused myself."*

Some women, more comfortable with their own sexuality, more secure in their ability to take care of themselves, sometimes set their own rules. They instigate sexually related discussions or behaviors, laugh at sexual jokes and join in the fray. While rare, some women with power in their own right in industries rife with sexual harassment are fighting fire with fire, fashioning their behavior after their male role models. A few women with power flaunt it; i.e., telling a vendor they will not buy from him unless he "takes her to bed first."

The Reservoir of Male Anger

The workplace is indeed in transition. Sexual harassment continues because of changing behaviors and views as well as the wellspring of anger that underpins both genders. Women, as recipients of most of the harassment, are ridding themselves of anger with the assistance of the law. Men, for the most part, have not cleansed themselves. Keith Russell Ablow, writer and chief resident in psychiatry at the New England Medical Center in Boston, addressed the dichotomy men face in a December 10, 1991, column in *The Washington Post*, entitled "Sexist Remarks: Tapping the Reservoir of Male Anger." Included here are selected pertinent paragraphs that explain the work environment and point to the reason for male anger.

> Nearly all the environments in which I have worked or studied, from college and medical school classrooms to hospitals, to media corporations, have included a masculine subculture—well educated

and genteel—that encourages views of women as sexually needy or confused, emotionally unbalanced and potentially self-destructive.

This masculine subculture has several related tenets. First, it holds that career motivation in a woman who does not temper her ambition with flirtation represents an abnormal displacement of sexual desire into occupational advancement. Second, it makes the case, often as a what-she-needs jest, that a woman's intellectual and professional energy can be quelled by providing her with good-enough sex. Third, it casts women as the unfortunate victims of unwieldy hormones likely responsible for displays of anger or stereotypically male toughness.

For men, membership in "the club" is frequently offered by senior staff members. They make clear, through their own off-color remarks, that the sexist posture of junior colleagues will place them in no real peril and may, in fact, make them one of the inner circle.

Dr. Ablow goes on to note the behavior of some women in response to this as:

... claiming an uneasy associate membership in the male subculture. They do so by making their own sexually derogatory remarks about themselves or other women. This lends an unfortunate air of credibility to the subculture's prejudices.

Ablow further describes the framework of the club:

In the dozens of back-room men's club gatherings to which I have been privy, no one has ever fully broken ranks with the group by strenuously objecting to the degradation of a woman.

The lack of vocal opposition is multifaceted. To many men, sexist remarks can read like tests of faith in that refusing the implied camaraderie will lead others to doubt their sexual prowess. Participating in this reduction of women to objects is offered as proof of manliness.

Dr. Ablow furnished speculation as to why male anger exists:

Some psychoanalysts would say that the need of some men to diminish females, particularly female authority figures, lies even deeper, in remnants of anger about the level of control exercised by their mothers. There may also be lingering frustration over maintaining intimacy without sexually consummating the mother-son relationship. It should come as no surprise, viewed through the lens of these theories, that off-hand sexual comments about powerful women can provoke giggling from 50-year-old men.

Another reservoir of male anger may be the traditional female role in screening potential sexual partners. The proper right of women to accept or refuse advances makes them instant authority figures. Women can say 'no.' This might partly explain the frequency with which men half-joke about female authority figures that 'she needs to be bent over the desk.'

Ablow ends by suggesting:

What seems clear is that these conscious and unconscious issues are pervasive and largely ignored. We know too little about the dynamics of sexism directed against women.

Dramatic hearings and stringent rules of decorum may change the landscape of male-female interactions, but, until we commit ourselves to full study of the underlying residual conflicts, they will continue to smolder underground.

Harassment—Who, Why and Where?

It is often believed that sexual harassment is about sexual attraction. For the most part it is not. As Dr. Ablow suggests, sexual harassment is about power, about preserving the status quo of male enclaves, about intimidation, about wrestling the internal conflicts residing in both genders.

Some sexual harassment is engaged in by males who want to *score*, perhaps to feed their male egos, show their prowess and keep in "the men's club"—doing what comes naturally without thinking about the ramifications. Men are predators. If they weren't, civilization might not be here today. Predatory instincts drive the propagation of the human race. According to Dr. Ablow, both the media and the workplaces perpetuate this behavior when they feed America with macho images or male self-identities. In the workplace, some men simply enjoy the game.

> *"I would try to ignore it but I do believe that there are a lot of men in the workforce who think they are superior to women."*

Other men with fragile egos appear to need reinforcement of their lovableness and/or their ability to protect the only roles they see for themselves—the main breadwinners or male predators. These men base their decisions upon what they see as their needs or their *divine rights* rather than on anticipating the effects of their actions. Such men have yet to learn the meaning of unwanted attention.

As women assume more power in organizations, insecure men can feel threatened. The more tightly they can control their environment, the more secure they feel. Thus many insecure men work hard at keeping women in their place. When they do this, they often react by relating to women in the only way they know—sexually. This is sexual harassment—or, power harassment expressed sexually.

Women also engage in power harassment as they attempt to gain or consolidate their gains and move upward in management positions. Power harassment takes other forms as well. It shows up as sex (gender) harassment, crude and intimidating behavior to keep the opposite gender in her/his place, but not expressed in sexual terms. An example of this type of behavior is when a person ignores or makes light of whatever the opposite gender individual says.

Gender harassment such as this is very prevalent in male-dominated environments in order to keep up the barriers to entry. Scenario 20—where the electrical utility crewman violated Ellen's space verbally and physically— illustrates this well.

Power harassment is common in workplaces, especially in environments where people wrestle for control. Often neither sexual nor gender directed, such power struggles may exist between males or between females who perceive another same sex individual as a real threat or someone they would simply like to eliminate from the competition. Women often see other women as adversaries for the perceived few slots they are allowed to fill. The formal name of the game is *politics*; i.e., deciding when to kow-tow or whom to eliminate. Politics, always a detriment to productivity, is not illegal. However, when *politics* emerges in harassing behavior, disadvantaging another because of her/his sex, it is sex discrimination, an actionable event.

"It's amazing to me what men think they can get away with."

Cases of sexual harassment occur when supervisors or members of management request sexual favors in exchange for favoritism, commonly referred to as *quid pro quo*. These individuals obviously misuse power. Very real but less obvious are instances wherein a more qualified female employee is denied a promotion in favor of a less qualified female who happens to be dating her supervisor, or when a female employee who refuses a social relationship of any type with her supervisor (such as drinks after work), is treated to any or a combination of many tactics. These include being denied promotions or pay raises, being assigned dirty jobs or less interesting work, or being given less advice and counsel. *More* and *less* are often difficult to prove.

A minority of sexual harassment events occur because a member of one sex is truly attracted to a member of the opposite sex, and the attraction is not reciprocal. These events escalate when neither the woman nor the man has learned how to acknowledge the attraction without belittling it, and are unable to move on to a more platonic relationship where the attraction is not allowed to dominate.

Age is not a factor in sexual harassment; power often grows as beauty lessens and competence increases. Perhaps the unresolved mother image takes over. Even grandmothers face harassment. Attractiveness plays a part when true sexual attraction (lust) is the impetus for harassment. However, looks are not critical. If a boss wants to keep his secretary performing work for him that she would not ordinarily do, striking up a personal relationship will often lock in her behavior, looks notwithstanding.

"I would not quit my job. It's just what he wants."

Women who become pioneers in a workplace; i.e., women who go first into male-dominated environments, face far more sexual harassment by males on a day-to-day basis than women in female-dominated environments, and vice versa. In male-dominated environments, membership in the "men's club" is an unwritten rule. Sexual (power) harassment to defend the turf is rife in the widest variety of predominately male environments, such as: the trades—road building, telephone installation, construction; money management—securities sales, options trading, investments; lucrative private partnerships—law, accounting, consulting; media—film, music, video, television, newspaper reporting; higher levels of government, academia and corporations, where women are kept from breaking through *the glass ceiling*.

Women working in educational institutions have shared that they believe more discrimination and sexual harassment occur in academia than in the corporate world. Uniquely, academics enjoy absolute independence, particularly if tenured, compared with employees elsewhere. In the interest of academic freedom, some faculty members often assume a *divine right of kings* mentality that they perceive puts them above and beyond the law. A similar power mentality is found sometimes at the highest levels of corporations and government: "with enough money and/or power I can do anything I want to do." Many of these excesses have surfaced in the last few years. Discrimination and harassment are no different than other issues, either in the top of corporations or government. Didn't Congress vote itself exempt from *Title VII*? Power!!!

Harassment—What and How?

Unfortunately, employers and employees rarely understand the full spectrum of behavior that constitutes harassment. Too often it is narrowly perceived simply as *quid pro quo*. The legal definition and the real range of events are much broader. As a result, management lacks an understanding of what constitutes a hostile work environment and how it negatively impacts people, productivity and profits.

GE Fanuc Automation North America, Inc. of Charlottesville, Virginia, a joint venture between General Electric Company and the Japanese firm Fanuc, provides a brochure and training to employees to prevent harassment in their environment. Their brochure depicts harassment visually as shown on page 80.

The degree of offensiveness increases from left to right on the chart. Columns one through three—visual, verbal and written—all describe unwanted attention, while columns four through seven describe invasion. Events from columns one through three would normally need to be repeated in order to qualify for investigation—possibly fitting a pattern and continuing after the victim has notified the harasser and management that the actions are unwelcome. Under normal conditions, one event from columns four through seven would precipitate investigation of the charge.

Some confusion might exist as to what these words really mean, how they are expressed in actions in workplace environments and how they are viewed by reasonable women. A review of selected scenarios from Part One will clarify a few points.

According to this chart, the managing partner (co-owner) in Scenario 3 verbally harassed with lewd comments and sexual references. They were patterned. Yet most of the women we surveyed considered the partner's behavior to be more highly offensive than simply crude language. Why? While he did not use his position to request dates or sex, he nevertheless held a relationship of power

Sexual Harassment
A Spectrum of Behavior Patterns

Visual	Verbal	Written	Touching	Power	Threats	Force
• Ogling	• Unwanted requests for dates	• Unwanted love poems	• Violating space	• Relationships	• Quid Pro Quo	• Rape
• Staring	• Questions about personal life	• Unwanted love letters	• Patting	• Using position to request dates, sex, etc.	• Demands	• Physical assault
• Posters	• Lewd comments	• Obscene poems	• Grabbing		• Loss of job	
• Magazines	• Dirty/sexual jokes	• Unwanted cards	• Pinching		• Selection process	
• Flyers	• Whistling		• Caressing			
			• Kissing			

Source: GE Fanuc Automation North America, Inc.

over Ellen. He controlled an environment that Ellen was powerless to change. Respondents felt degraded, a position few women will allow to continue. Thus, most women in this survey chose as their course of action to "quit the job." This shows much farther to the right on the spectrum and could be considered a *quid pro quo*. Respondents chose not to waste their time filing a charge that they no doubt believed to be "iffy." However, when viewed in the light of *quid pro quo*, they may make different choices in the future. In the meantime, women surveyed voiced loud and clear that they would not continue working for anyone so lacking in respect.

Scenarios 23—the "stand up and show your fanny" event, and 24—flowers to the "gals"— point out the differences when members of management act.

> *"When having problems with one individual, something can be done, but when an entire organization—including top management—has an attitude problem—I feel less can be done."*

Almost all women were understandably offended that a member of management would either in private or in public tell a woman to display her fanny. While the manager made only one sexual comment (column two), it was stated as an order. The manager was seen as not only extremely insensitive, but also as a definite authority figure with power over individual women. In the "men's club" that women know about, this manager has the power to share whatever comments he wishes about Ellen in private to other men, including their current management. Women felt degraded and further realized this action placed them in a no-win situation. It is unwise to embarrass a superior in your company, regardless of his or her actions.

When the vice president sent all women flowers and notes, however, most women in the survey perceived the event as annoying rather than degrading. The unwanted cards and gifts were viewed on the left-hand side of the spectrum. Respondents did not view this situation as a threat from an authority figure, but rather the act of a man hopelessly behind the times. There was no perception of individual danger. (The only danger expressed had to do with whether the man is really bright enough to keep the company "in the black.")

In Scenario 5, the "what did the rapist eat for breakfast" situation, women perceived a wide range of degrees of offensiveness.

Some women passed off the comment as a dirty/sexual joke, often heard. Some even checked "inoffensive" and "used to it." Others claimed annoyance. Still others, however, stated this comment's offensiveness as 10, and checked intimidated and degraded. "Individual perceptions of women vary . . . However, they share common concerns." When women viewed this remark as coming from the mind of a warped man, the kind of man who talks about committing physical acts, or so insensitive to the threat of violence women face, they cared not to be associated with him at all. Many events annoy women, but when they feel degraded, at risk or both, they consider the degree of offensiveness much higher.

In order to understand why women vary in their responses, it is important to understand the concept of individual "comfort zones" as they apply to harassment.

COMFORT ZONES

Don Thoren, President of Phoenix-based Thoren Consulting Group, describes a *comfort zone* as a circle one draws around oneself to allow inside those behaviors with which they are comfortable. These behaviors are their own or, reciprocally, behaviors of others that they will accept without considering the comments or actions offensive. Falling outside the individual *comfort zone* are comments and actions that are viewed as offensive. The wider the circle, the more comfortable an individual is with a broader range of behaviors.

Each person has a different comfort zone. Likewise, each person selects what she/he puts inside the zone, for whom, when and why. In other words, people have different comfort zones for different individuals with whom they interact.

"Reactions to touching are very dependent on personalities, situation and intent."

For example, a male business associate may tell a woman, "You really look nice in that outfit," and, depending upon her relationship with the man, she might feel complimented. She allows that inside her comfort zone giving the man permission to discuss her person for one of several reasons. This may be because he has treated her with respect in the past, she views him as safe (non-threatening) or, at the other end of the spectrum,she may be attracted to him.

Another male associate may make the same comment and the same woman may put it outside the comfort zone and feel offended. She may feel uncomfortable with that male and want no personal comments from him.

As a comparison, if either of the two male associates had stated their thoughts in another way; i.e., "you really fill out that outfit," the woman addressed would, in almost all cases, put the comment outside the comfort zone and be offended. Such a comment refers to a woman's intimate body parts and violates her space.

Scenario 7—the Ellen, Joe and Bob story (Ellen flirted with Joe, making Bob feel that he was welcome to be more familiar with her) illustrates how and why individuals change who and what they will allow into their comfort zones.

Ellen moved Bob outside her zone when he began to make her uncomfortable, violating her personal space and dictating his feelings of love, which were not mutual.

In order to help visualize the concept of comfort zones, refer to the chart on page 84.

Every woman has a tolerance for remarks she believes to be offensive, depending upon her morals and tempered by the reality of her stress level. With these in mind, she allows comments and actions into her comfort zone. Most women find far more remarks offensive than they allow to show. Yet, one can only hold so much anger within. Many women keep too much anger inside; others have learned to write off remarks and actions toward them in order to keep their stress levels manageable.

Survey respondents selected for one single scenario, an "offensive" action, their reaction as "annoyed," and when asked what action they would take they chose, "ignore it," for situations such as a congressman kissing an employee on the cheek or a boorish manager commenting on how "her husband was taking good care of her." Such women no longer attempt to reform the world or rid it of jerks. Consciously or unconsciously, they realize the cost to their stress levels and refuse to react, thus appearing to move some offensive comments and actions into their comfort zones. To survive, many women have adopted an ancient maxim herein expressed as they often hear it from their male colleagues: *Illigitemi Non*

Comfort Zones
Degree of Offensiveness   Action or Comments

Outside the Comfort Zone

Offensive	Sexually explicit pictures
Offensive	"What a pair of knockers"
Offensive	Pinching one's buttocks
Offensive	"You really fill out that outfit!"

Potential Comfort Zone

Possibly Offensive	A warm hug for a job well done
Possibly Offensive	"You look great in that outfit!"

Comfort Zone

Almost never	"What a beautiful necklace!"
Almost never	"How about lunch? I'm starved!"

Possibly Offensive	"How about a long lunch to talk about the project, then we'll work late to finish it up and I'll drop you off at home?"
Probably Offensive	"I hear they caught the rapist today…I'd like to ask him what he eats for breakfast."

Offensive	Continued use of four-letter obscenities.
Offensive	References to women as "broads, bimbos."
Offensive	Remarks such as, "Your husband is taking good care of you, isn't he?"

Carborundum "Don't let the bastards grind you down." This is particularly true of women who choose to survive in male-dominated work environments, but, they do *not* like that choice.

WHAT THE LAW DID NOT ACCOMPLISH

An existing culture does not change by legislation. If anything, an attempt at dramatic change breeds hostility and revolution. The fact that the law changed in 1964 did not change the actions of women or men. Women given new opportunities rarely sought them or accepted them when offered. They did not set aside their own prejudices, and therefore did not invite hostility or revolution.

In one example, seven years after passage of the *Civil Rights Act* women refused promotions into so-called men's jobs. During an aggressive hiring period at a clean, high-tech assembly plant, 10 to 15 new assemblers were needed in job codes previously referred to as *men's work*. Approximately 1,000 women were employed as assemblers at lower pay rates and approximately 100 men were employed as assemblers at higher pay rates. Prior to the change in the law, management would have ignored upgrading women and simply hired men as new assemblers. The law suddenly made that practice illegal. Management thought that senior women assemblers would jump at the chance for the higher paying positions. The women were asked, in order of seniority, to fill these positions. Six hundred women were contacted before the first woman accepted an upgrade. The law gave them permission to accept, but the women's mindsets did not. They still viewed these positions as men's work.

In 1986, Barbara F. Reskin and Heidi I. Hartman edited an extensive study concerning sex segregation on the job. In their work, *Women's Work, Men's Work* (National Academy Press), they point out that as late as 1981, more than 62 percent of employed men and women would have to exchange jobs in the workforce in order for sex role segregation to be abolished. Despite the feminist movement and the need for women to enter and remain in the workforce today, that percentage dropped less than 10 percentage points in 1990. More than *one-half* of the workforce participants would have to exchange jobs to abolish sex role stereotyping.

"Genetically inferior! He obviously believes women are only equipped with one thing and it's NOT a brain."

You can legislate behavior, but you cannot legislate thoughts or mindsets. Neither has the law legislated away the "men's club" atmosphere and verbal degradation of women as *rites of passage* out of their hearing, where they cannot counteract it. Nothing in the law forced women into men's roles. It simply protected their rights to choose. Although the law protected them from the subtleties they face in male-dominated work environments: profanity, off-color jokes, gossip about their personal life, anecdotes about male prowess and intimacy toward them, it has been slow to affect positive changes in employee climates.

Values are a product of early childhood, education and environment. Children are given sex-related toys, expectations and role models. The *men as predator* philosophy emerges in early elementary school as boys chase and kiss girls but run when girls chase them for the same reason. In many pre-school and kindergarten classes today, girls still play with dolls in one corner while boys play with trucks in another. Studies show that boys are treated as more serious students and given more attention by teachers in grade school, even though the majority of elementary school teachers are women. Fortunately, in some enlightened elementary school districts, new programs are in place to force conscious revision of these behaviors.

Beliefs build upon each other and dictate choices. Often beliefs and values result in prejudices and even discrimination. Prejudice is an internal phenomenon that entails making judgments based upon insufficient evidence, such as "Women don't make good CEOs." Discrimination is the result of prejudice and is an external action directed either in favor of or against someone. Discrimination is illegal; prejudice—or holding beliefs—is not. However, prejudice must be viewed as the systemic problem and treated before wholesale reversal of discrimination can occur. Since prejudice is a *learned response*, albeit deeply ingrained, it can be *unlearned*. Some beliefs simply are so deeply ingrained that much prejudice has not been unlearned, evidence of its validity notwithstanding.

> *"I am often asked about my husband's job within the context of my profession and am always frustrated to think that I am viewed as his baggage."*

Women and men have not exchanged information sufficiently to break down the barriers of age-old stereotypes and prejudices. Neither the law nor employers can legislate mindsets, but the law has provided further assistance. The "reasonable woman concept" suggests that men base their behaviors on a new perspective: a view of the world from the mind of the victim. Hopefully, if this transformation takes place, all individuals will treat others of varying ethnicity or age groups with similar concern.

A challenge? Absolutely! Men and women have held different views across the board throughout history. Only extraordinary communication can bring about an understanding of these differences. In addition, many views women hold are both particular to each woman and in a state of flux. Commonalities do exist, however. Women do not like to be intimidated, degraded or violated. Can both genders sort through and stop the actions that cause these feelings? No one thought the Berlin Wall would come down, or Communism would fail. The law did not mandate their demise. When they became a hindrance rather than a help to accomplish mutual goals, they collapsed. Perhaps a focus on mutual goals will aid this process.

Both sexual and sex harassment are sex discrimination, by law and in fact. Victims find it more difficult to accomplish assigned work and maintain healthy levels of stress as they fight power and intimidation. They operate at less than peak performance. With biases in place, victims are promoted less often, forced to quit their jobs more often, and many women victims choose not to enter the male-dominated environments that pay significantly greater financial rewards. A closer look at these issues may promote an understanding of the true costs of harassing behaviors.

Chapter Four

The Real Costs of Discrimination

THE EFFECTS OF HARASSMENT AND DISCRIMINATION

Sex discrimination is war—*civil war*—and harassment appears to be the weapon of choice. In the sex discrimination war, one segment of the American population attempts to force its views and beliefs upon another segment, views no longer appropriate to this culture at this time. Hopefully, American business, the professions, academia and government will realize the real costs and carnage of this war and help to end it.

It is important to keep in mind that the U.S. is simultaneously fighting another war: meeting the challenge of global competition. The war of discrimination makes the cost of the global competitive war even more expensive and America's place in the world economy more perilous.

The Effects of Harassment and Discrimination on Employees

The effects of sex discrimination on employees, with or without sexually harassing behaviors, falls into three main categories: the physical, the psychological and the economic.

The Physical... While some discriminatory and harassing behaviors include physical assault with bodily harm, most workplace events do not. However, job discrimination in hiring or promotions, or hostile workplaces produces real illnesses in victims. Common complaints include headaches and ulcers. When problems are not solved or workplaces not changed, more serious stress-related diseases can develop. During periods of very high stress, even the brightest individuals and most dynamic managers find themselves unable to function normally or make even simple decisions. Real illnesses incur costs to the victim's long-term health and well-being. Beyond that, they can lead to psychological and economic losses for victims living in fear of impaired health and a continued inability to function; the possibility of lost wages; and medical bills for treatment. Over time, stress-related diseases can debilitate victims.

"For self-preservation, I've just had to let a lot of these comments go."

Many women voted to "ignore" situations, even though they expressed annoyance or anger at events in many scenarios. Some women will ignore these; many will allow the feelings to fester. Often these feelings start the chain that leads to stress-related illnesses.

Normal, healthy sexual attraction exists in workplaces. Often it's *okay*. But, when it doesn't feel *okay*, women are learning to say "no," and take some action. They shouldn't ignore uncomfortable situations. In the long run, taking some action pays off in better health.

The Psychological... Victims often experience fear and anxiety as the result of traumatic experiences. They fear bodily harm, anticipate loss of their jobs and feel a sense of failure. This leaves an inaccurate impression with their employer and/or peers. Sometimes they are forced to take actions that further disadvantage them within their worksites, and both resentment and anxiety build. Personal danger and job security become real issues.

When discriminatory or harassing events occur—and sometimes long afterward—victims often suffer gut-wrenching emotions that range from simple embarrassment, to full-fledged anger at themselves and/or the harasser, to feelings of degradation. Many women can recall visually and with anguish events that took place 20 to 30 years previously. "It's still there." Often, victims assume guilt inappropriately for some of the events. Whenever women and minorities lose in the workplace, they also lose self-esteem and self-respect. Guilt only exacerbates this problem.

"I would not have been able to handle this at all."

Discriminatory practices and hostile environments frequently result in victims quitting jobs. When these victims move out into the job market, they may now be doubly disadvantaged. Traumatized from past events, they may face a discriminatory interview environment with lowered self-esteem. Their lack of confidence often comes through in the interview and they may reenter the work environment at positions below their capabilities. As with stress, emotional trauma often leads to physical illness.

The Economic . . . Real illnesses cost dollars in lost wages and medical bills to employees, but economic concerns exist beyond these. When people are angry or stressed, they rarely perform at their peak. Continued harassment or perceived discrimination often affects job performance and real promotional opportunities. Discussions with peers to handle anger and solve problems impact productivity or increase workloads for victims. These may result in either voluntary or involuntary job changes. When they become the *last in,* during layoffs, they usually become the *first out.* Often women are forced to exit an entire industry where blatant sexual harassment occurs in order to maintain their self-respect. Normally these are industries and positions with higher (male) pay. Transfers and unwanted turnover rarely advantage women.

"Keep in mind you need your job."

Outright job discrimination allows few women to contribute in positions that shatter any glass ceilings where employees are richly rewarded for their abilities and contributions. Real dollar injustices do occur. When women attempt to play ball at higher levels of organizations, they are normally excluded from the "men's club," often given staff jobs and often provided with less information. It's difficult to support a team when you don't know the plays, difficult to support a manager when you don't know why. Without networks and information, women more frequently *fumble the ball* and are not viewed as team players. A December 30, 1991 *Wall Street Journal* article, reported how few women make it to the top. The percentage of women officers is over 4.1 percent only in apparel and publishing—industries heavily populated with women.

All forms of discrimination—including sexual harassment—impede the progress of women and minorities toward economic equality and freedom of options. This directly impacts autonomy and social equality as well. Discrimination has no place in a society where law supports economic equality, including the right of women to desexualize their economic livelihood.

The Effects of Harassment and Discrimination on Employers

Harassment and discrimination impact all employers economically, and some costs are more visible than others (although even visible costs can be overlooked by employers).

Hidden Costs . . . Lowered productivity exacts a high toll. Stress and emotional distress use mental and physical energies that could be focused on the job. This, combined with time spent in the rumor mill and avoidance of a harasser or hostile work environment, erode productivity and employee morale. Telling an employee to walk around the engineering department and the manufacturing plant instead of through it several times a day is hardly productive.

Power games, including withholding information from key players, whether directed at women or men, exact high costs. The workplace is rife with games that impact productivity and impede operations. In Scenario 49, the manager could not send his "rookie" on the road or to key clients—an excellent example of how power games cause real costs to escalate when a highly compensated victim is prevented from succeeding. Managers who are busy performing a job other than their own run organizations poorly, if at all. The costs of recruiting to replace employees failed by management, and the true costs of learning curves and training must be incurred twice.

Insulting remarks impact teamwork as well as productivity, further skewing business results. A manager who insults a women by insinuating that her husband provides for her should not expect this patronized employee to *follow him over the hill* when he needs her. Further, she will discuss his boorishness with peers. When a lack of teamwork is accompanied by an *idea shut out*, significant costs result. A woman who shares her ideas about an ad campaign directed to women and is not taken seriously by her male peers, may choose to leave, or she may choose to stay and engage in infighting, producing neither timely nor quality work. Since hers is the only viewpoint representing the customer, the ad campaign stands a good chance of being less successful.

America has not measured the loss of ideas from the female gender, but when ignored, whole industries can suffer. For example, engineering departments in the Big Three Auto Makers are hardly female environments. The Big Three did not lose out to the Japanese only because of quality. Detroit designed quality cars for 6' males weighing 200 pounds. The Japanese designed quality cars that fit 5'5" women who weigh less than 200 pounds—quality cars in which women can sit comfortably with back support and still reach the pedals. Today, the Japanese still provide a range of cars sized to a woman across a range of affordability. Women buy more than 50 percent of the cars in the United States. Their body sizes more typically match the Japanese buyer of either sex. Perhaps male dominance has cost American business real profits. If American industry wishes to sell to women and the Japanese, perhaps they could benefit from the ideas of both genders.

"I'd like to take my great sales record and look for a new job . . . ."

The ultimate in power harassment is directed at individuals who are perceived as threats; i.e., individuals willing to express their own ideas, individuals who are bright and noble competitors. In these games, the best and the brightest often are washed out by insecure managers who currently hold turf and power. Who is best suited to handle responsibility in any organization...the insecure, the F.O.s (friends of), or the best and the brightest regardless of gender? Power games enact very high costs as ideas and talent walk out the door. Employers who continue to allow the *old boy network* to dominate and to pick the successive *old boy network* will face not only this attrition but also increasingly negative publicity. Recruitment of the best and the brightest may be even more difficult.

Visible Costs . . . Loss of talent occurs at all levels of organizations as harassment and discrimination foster attrition. Skilled workers are at a premium today and will no longer tolerate an environment such as the one described in Scenario 45—the electronic technicians regaling the break room with soap opera bimbo stories and peppering the workplace with bikini-clad posters.

While managing language in break rooms is difficult, and females as well as males are guilty of crude behavior, removing posters and providing sexual harassment training for all employees will change expectations of behavior. Respect for individuals may have changed the decision of the woman in Scenario 22 who was accosted in the file room and reprimanded by the personnel manager in front of others for an offhand comment. She chose not even to return from lunch.

When employers have invested in good employees, they lose real dollars: costs of recruiting, costs of training and cost of lost productivity during another learning curve. The loss of real talent only compounds the costs.

All employers are now conscious of the escalating costs of medical care. Prevention of illness is touted in workplaces through diet, exercise and smoke-free environments. Some employers now furnish health clubs on the property or memberships in clubs. Yet, stress-related illnesses due to harassment have not been viewed similarly. When stress or emotional ailments disturb victims of the workplace, they are often viewed as personal rather than work-related problems. Many are personal problems that harassing workforce behaviors only exacerbate. Others stem directly from harassing and discriminatory treatment. These stressors often turn into physical illnesses, lost productivity and high medical costs.

"If the situation did not improve I would quit and contact the EEO."

As human resources counselors, the authors of this book have witnessed the dramatic changes in behavior and performance that occur when happy, productive employees suddenly report to new managers who prevent their previously superior or even acceptable performance through harassing or discriminatory behaviors. The view that surfaces upward is, "This employee can no longer cut it." Or, "This employee went off the deep end! Personal problems!" Yet, nothing in their personal lives changed, only their management. Employers rarely challenge these views, and in the past, employees rarely fought situations of this type. Increasingly, however, employees are recognizing discriminatory and harassing behaviors for what they are and turning to management for assistance.

No one ever fought an inexpensive lawsuit. With sexual harassment out of the closet, women will discuss actions with peers, file more lawsuits and turn to class action suits if their concerns are not addressed—all costly actions! One of the choices offered to women participating in this survey was: "Discuss confidentially with member of management." Many women struck the word "confidentially" from the text before checking it. Some women added words such as, "I'd tell everyone I know," "He doesn't deserve confidentiality," or "Everyone deserves to know about him."

Scenario 39 provides an excellent example of outrageous and libelous behavior when men placed messages in public view in vending machines to hassle a woman who was doing a good job. In yesterday's world, an employee who faced this simply lived in fear of finding the messages and "died in private" when she did, too embarrassed to mention it to anyone. Today, an employee facing this would photograph the unwelcome graffiti, keep a log of the events and present the case to management. If the graffiti did not stop, she would see a lawyer.

While most women voting on the scenarios chose to initially attempt to solve problems internally except for highly offensive events, at least one woman out of 100 would seek outside assistance in all but three of the scenarios presented and deemed offensive by more than 15 percent of the women. No one chose to request assistance over a nude on top a cake, a congressman who hasn't learned he can't kiss women as easily as babies, or a man touching a woman's shoulder while training her on the CRT. In every other instance, expect some action from someone—even if you mean well and award Bulls-Lakers tickets to your winners or send flowers to all the *gals* in your organization.

The personal and economic waste of legal pursuits through misunderstanding on the part of management was highlighted in *Corporate Attractions* by Kathleen Neville, Acropolis Books, Ltd., 1990, when she related the story of a woman who reported a sexual harassment incident to management. Even though her employer had a policy in place, the manager did not notify the general manager of her complaint, did not consult the company attorney and did not find a quick solution. The bottom line cost to all involved was $500,000 and seven years.

K-Mart probably did not foresee its $3.2 million settlement of a sexual harassment case in 1987, or perhaps they would have made different choices at the time. To these visible costs should be added the hidden costs of negative publicity and lowered employee productivity and morale.

> **"Lodging a complaint may make him think twice before he does it to another employee."**

Many employers risk lawsuits without fully understanding their financial impact, believing instead that they are making financially prudent decisions. Often employers hear accusations against a key employee whose dollar contribution to the company can be measured. They then look at that dollar amount as critical to maintaining their profit level and refuse to take action to change his/her behavior. This is extremely short-sighted, and if it was imprudent in the past, it's even more so today. With the passage of the *1991 Civil Rights Bill*, sexual harassment in some cases can be viewed as intentional and thus subject to compensatory and punitive damages, as well as jury trials. No one wins a lawsuit. The strain takes its toll in stress levels and real dollars. While sexual harassment training is not free, its costs are miniscule compared to the cost of one lawsuit.

The Effects of Harassment and Discrimination on the Nation

By the end of 1992, three major economic powers will dominate the world: The Pacific Rim, The European Economic Community and the United States of America. Does the U.S.want to be number three in this competitive triumvirate—falling behind not only in quality, but in gross national product and profits? Hopfully not, but low productivity, medical and legal costs eat at real profits, while misuse of talent and ideas takes a further toll.

"This is so archaic, it's hard to believe it's still happening."

Implicit in this country's challenge to compete is the assimilation of a culturally diverse workforce to meet the needs of "Workforce 2000." In Workforce *2000* , the U.S. Department of Labor states that between now and the year 2000, 64 percent of new entrants into the workforce will be women: 42 percent native white women, 13 percent native non-white women and 9 percent immigrant women. In addition, lower skilled jobs will decline and higher skilled jobs will increase. To utilize the American talent base, employers must address cultural diversity issues and provide workplaces that promote mutual respect. To do so, employers will be required to view women in roles other than traditional; ie, as craftspersons, engineers, lawyers, executives, not wives, mothers, girlfriends and daughters. Managements would be well advised to join in the movement to stop sex discrimination in all forms and become allies of both women and minorities to meet the cultural diversity challenge of Workforce 2000

Chapter Five

The Challenge of Changing the Workplace

THE CHALLENGE EMPLOYERS FACE

The impact of ongoing change reverberates today as visible technological and political changes stun the world. American business, academia and government pore over data and exchange ideas as they wrestle to understand these changes and manage within them. Concurrently, less obvious economic and social changes fester with less insight. Yet, structuring economic and social change is as implicit to the survival of every American as developing technological opportunities and structuring peaceful political boundaries.

Lester Thurow, Dean, Sloan School of Management, Massachussetts Institute of Technology, spoke concisely to these issues in a 1991 address:

> The key things affecting the American economy in the next decade are basically going to be things which are determined by somebody sitting somewhere else in the world—not by somebody sitting in Washington, D.C.
>
> If you think about it, you will see that this is a revolution and not an evolution. The problems with economic revolutions, as opposed to political revolutions, is that often they are not obvious. Then, the question is how to gear yourself up and make the changes you have to make.
>
> We have a very simple bottom line for the 1990s. If you want to succeed, you will have to change. If you really want to succeed, you've got to change before you have to change. And, if you're going to change before you have to change, the question is how to get human beings involved in an organization to change the corporate culture—to be willing to do the things they have to do.

A challenge? Yes. Meeting the challenge that Thurow suggests requires change on three fronts: *Legal*—becoming aware of and complying with new laws; *Economic*—meeting global competition; and *Cultural*—blending a mixed-gender, mixed-racial workforce with mutual respect and enhanced productivity.

On the Legal Front—New realities of the 1990s suggest a different approach to the law: seriousness about compliance. First, economics will continue to force women into the workplace. As the law increasingly protects the economic well being of women and minorities, and as tax dollars for social programs lessen, these groups will become more vocal. Votes and comments on the scenarios presented to the survey respondents clearly indicate that women will speak up and fight back, physically or legally, to protect their incomes. They will not ignore insults as in the past or gloss over patronizing comments. They will become full-fledged participants in the workforce, with the force of the law behind them.

On the Economic Front—In the past, most people applied the word *competitive* to business; i.e., a *dog-eat-dog world*. Professors in academia, counselors in the professions and statesmen in government stood above that fray. Being more monopolistic and bureaucratic, public sectors did not feel the pinch. Today, Americans across the board understand the need for contained costs in all areas to ensure America's economic survival. Medical care has changed dramatically; education is under scrutiny. Congress is under attack. Institutions that do not police their own ethics and costs now face irate taxpayers and judges willing to assist them in the courts of law. Global competition, with its new cost-cutting mentality, will slice away at all previously protected expenditures.

On the Cultural Front—Americans now expect everyone to work—even mothers of small children. Women and minorities will continue to move into higher paying technical and professional positions across all industries and work groups; i.e., engineers, electronics technicians, doctors, skilled workers, film directors, and investment counsellors. Almost 30 percent of the workforce will be nonwhite by the year 2000. A total reform of institutions and practices is required, including new ideas, new products, new services, renewed respect for the individual. Discrimination and sexual harassment now must be viewed as impediments to needed social change.

The current rallying cry for social change within the workplace is "empowerment." With the realization that restructuring, downsizing, de-layering, et al., did not achieve the desired competitive objectives, managements are now tapping people power, the secret ingredient of competitiveness.

Empowerment is shared influence and control. It is not something that management gives or delegates. It is something employees own by nature. The good news about empowerment is the growth of self-directed work and the demise of unnecessary layers of management. American employers are capitalizing on the vast talent potential of American employees to create the greatest tool of competitiveness.

"I wonder how our system would react if the tables were turned and men became the victims."

If women and minorities are to be empowered, self or otherwise, the culture of the organization must meet their needs for self-respect, personal achievement and recognition as individuals in order for them to contribute toward common employer goals. Responding to supply and demand, women and minorities will have the luxury of seeking and finding employers—and educational institutions—where cultures allow them to reach their fullest potential. They will do so. Holistic treatment will become a major bargaining chip of these populations during the 1990s.

Looking abroad at countries where sexual harassment and discrimination still flourish, it might be easy to shrug off the importance of solving basic problems within this milieu. After all, many foreign countries still produce high quality, competitive products without the U.S.'s concern for discrimination. Expectations differ here. American consciousness has been raised; social change will not stop impacting American employees; i.e., its human resources. The challenge of every employer to compete is to manage and use ideas and resources. The chemical composition of physical resources, their integral properties and boundaries, are well understood. Employers must understand the integral psychological properties and boundaries of people—human resources—and provide a climate for these resources to flourish.

"I would not work where I was not taken seriously and treated with respect."

To survive, employers might consider returning to *psychological contracts.* As discussed in *Managing Organizational Behavior* by Schermerhorn, Hunt and Osborn, a psychological contract is less formal than a written union contract dealing with pay and benefits. Instead, it spells out a set of expectations on the part of both employer and employee specifying what each will give and expect from the other. In short, it describes the working relationship based upon mutual respect.

Individuals offer contributions such as: effort, time, creativity, cooperation, and commitment to the organization. In turn, organizations offer: respect, opportunity, fringe benefits, and pay. This could be termed a positive *quid pro quo.* Managers ensure that the fair exchange of values continues. An organization that allows discrimination and/or harassment weakens or negates the contract.

Unfortunately, just when this country's leaders are most in need, American people least trust their leaders. *Beyond The Trust Gap,* Horton and Reid, Business One/Irwin, 1991, speaks to the loss of trust between senior and middle managers caused by downsizings of organizations during the past few years. Horton and Reid espouse a return to loyalty through commitment, respect and shared goals if America will continue to compete globally. Solid management must underpin an organization to provide for continued success. The psychological contract encourages individuals at all levels of an organization to contribute and ensure that success.

Success means meeting the overriding challenge: changing corporate (employer) cultures to make America competitive. On the legal front, the mandate is specific and clear. On the economic front, the hunt to ferret out all unnecessary costs pervades every arena. On the cultural front, understanding of the challenge is now only beginning to emerge. Employers must understand and manage their human resources and replace lost productivity by team development and empowerment of all employees. To do this, employers must replace "accommodation" of women and minorities with respect. This will end the sex discrimination war.

CULTURAL CHANGE—WHAT STAYS, WHAT GOES, WHAT COMES

Knowing what to change is difficult enough; implementing change successfully is even more of a challenge. Most human beings initially resist change. Under stress, change is resisted even more and there is retreat into a comfortable past. However, when people affiliate with others who are undergoing the change, they face less risk and less fear. Thus, workplaces that take a strong stand on effecting the change will produce greater results.

Perceptions

Before creating a dynamic workplace with employee relationships based upon mutual respect, undesirable prejudices and behaviors must be ferreted out and changed. Prejudice continues because of outdated perceptions that must be set aside. Deeply ingrained religious beliefs and customs in many countries have kept women in positions subordinate to men. *The Old Testament*, the *Koran*, and St. Paul's beliefs in *The New Testament*, all describe the preeminence of men in the eyes of God. The role models from past generations, both male and female, expressed these beliefs in their choices and behavior patterns. Some of these beliefs are:

A woman's natural place is in the home.

A woman committed to job rather than family is "unwomanly."

Women lack reason and are governed by emotion.

Women should be subordinate to men.

Women are not tough-minded. Men need to take care of them.

Because of this religious and cultural background, *nice* men still tend to view and treat *nice* women as mothers, wives, sisters, daughters; i.e., dependents of someone, not as intellectual and/or professional equals. They have learned to interact with women in a personal rather than professional way. Such men do not see themselves as harassers of women, even though they unwittingly are if they treat a woman personally when professional treatment is more appropriate. When men view women as nice, rather than as equals, they close their eyes to the reality of sexual harassment. Women become daughters, not proteges, screened out of opportunities and demeaned by condescension. The *old boys' network* rarely includes women, as women are little understood. The "men's club" maintains the distance. Rarely do women receive promotional opportunities they deserve; rarely do they receive valid mentoring.

> *"I'd discuss how frustrating these outdated views were and that I don't want my life run by others' hang-ups."*

In viewing personal relationships between men and women, several more myths stand out:

- Only attractive women get harassed.
- Women who get harassed are asking for it.
- Men don't get harassed.
- Sexual harassment doesn't happen to managers and executives.
- Promiscuity leads to sexual harassment.
- Most sexual harassment happens only in "women's minds."
- Women charge sexual harassment when they are in trouble on the job.

Evidence abounds that these are indeed myths. But, taking a shortcut to the heart of the matter, harassment is too pervasive to believe these myths. As perceptions, however, they perpetuate the belief that sexual harassment is a women's problem rather than a business problem. The law regulates behavior with regard to this business problem as clearly as it regulates anti-trust actions, insider selling and toxic waste disposal. In response to these, companies set clear rules for employees to follow, regardless of their personal ethical beliefs. And so it is with sexual harassment and discrimination. Hopefully, companies will help managers and employees to shape new and concerned attitudes toward solving these problems. In the interim, companies must institute policies and practices, and monitor them as they would any other business issue. How strong your policy, how strict your monitoring will determine if the business problem becomes bigger, smaller or goes away.

Some perceptions of the past, now viewed as outmoded, compound the difficulty of solving other business problems. These views direct behavior inappropriately in the workplace. The following perceptions, behaviors and practices are now illegal:

- The assumption that turnover rate is higher among women than men.

- Beliefs that men are less capable of assembling pieces of intricate equipment.
- Beliefs that women are less capable of aggressive salesmanship.
- State laws restricting hours, overtime pay, lifting requirements. (All of these have been superseded by the *Civil Rights Act.*)
- Seniority systems that maintain separate lines of progression and displacement for males and females.
- Job posting or advertising that specifies male or female.
- Discrimination regarding fringe benefits.
- Policies and practices that discriminate against women because of pregnancy, childbirth or related medical conditions.

When employers maintain perceptions such as these, job segregation continues. Women are not encouraged to move outside of *women's work*, nor are they evaluated fairly when they do. Male-dominated environments continue to flourish with blatant sex discrimination and harassment. Women as well as men must change their perceptions about what is really *men's work* and *women's work*. Women must be able to leave the *pink ghetto* if that is what they wish. In order to accomplish this successfully, the "men's club" must fold.

"Hopefully, there would be at least one mature male in the crowd that would stand up for her . . . ."

Perceptions of the past exist in many sexist remarks ongoing in the workplace. Either purposefully—to keep women in their place—or without conscious thought, they perpetuate the "men's club." Who will speak out to bring forth its demise? To break cultural barriers, it is necessary to start at the top. Those with less to fear and more ability to impact can set new cultural mores: Degrading any employee is no longer allowed; respect for all individuals is now expected.

Looking at the world differently; i.e., a new world view, will help individuals to implement these new mores. First, we must look at facts rather than myths. In the reality of the 1990s, women must work most of their lives. Few have a choice. No longer is the *proper* role of women necessarily in the home. No longer are women properly wives and daughters first and people second. They are people first. Unfortunately, most interaction with women by men has been based upon perceptions, not upon evaluation of their real experiences with women. Men now must evaluate these experiences rather than predicating their beliefs and behavior on outdated stereotypes.

The challenge is clear but the task is not easy. The gender gap is a deeply rooted value system that sees women as inferior to men. This must change. Old role models are dead; new ones must be created en route to Workforce 2000.

FEMALE BEHAVIOR

Perceptions and beliefs, including prejudices, direct behavior. Women are not without guilt in accepting male role models and/or some outdated stereotypes that determine their behavior. These surface in a variety of relationships.

In women-to-women relationships, some women play power games with other women such as withholding information, possibly following male role models in getting ahead, or feeding egos and protecting turfs. Competition for the few slots near the top can drive some women to discredit others. Any behavior of this type between women debases the image women need as professionals, regardless of their positions in the hierarchical structure or their classification of work. When women fight women, either overtly or covertly, all women lose. And, they only reinforce stereotypes, invalid as they might be.

Women hold different standards and expectations for other women as managers. Often they expect women to be fairer, more under-standing of their personal problems, stronger in relationship build-ing than male peers. Isn't that what the stereotype says? Must women hold superior expectations and then withdraw support when women fail to meet these superior standards of perfection?

"And women wonder why men act the way they do!"

Scenario 15 sheds light upon another behavior pattern that must be addressed. A cake in the shape of a nude women offended more than 60 percent of the survey respondents. Many other women voted it inoffensive because "it was women who did it." Does being a woman excuse sexual harassment of males, embarrassment of other female co-workers or crude behavior? A few perceptive women shared comments that showed that they saw this for what it really was: sexual harassment of a male by females. In many work groups, such sexual displays continue at the instigation of women. Yet, if women wish sexual harassment to stop, they must also stop harassing males and other females. They must not promote a "double standard." Most women today wish to be treated as professionals. Nudity will not break down sex role stereotyping; crudity will not earn respect.

One respondent, an assembler in a manufacturing plant in the Northeast who was offended by the cake and photo scenes, wrote an attachment to the evaluations, as follows:

> I believe that no matter the position you are in, you should handle yourself as a lady. I know there are men and women out there who have no respect for an individual and their beliefs. We have lost respect for each other. No wonder our leaders are lost. How can they make it a better place to live when we can't do it for ourselves . . .

Lady is a term of respect. Many women today believe the term lady is too limiting, portraying them in traditional roles of wife, mother, daughter. Thus they reject this title. This view may be shortsighted. Respect is the glue needed today to build working relationships that are neither sexually driven nor gender based. *Lady* is a non-sexual term, on a par with *gentleman*, a term of respect. Harassment is the lack of respect. If women wish to earn respect and stop harassment; i.e., eliminate the *boys will be boys behavior*, then *girls will be girls* behavior must also be eliminated. Must women bristle when called a lady? In fact, defining the term lady in a professional sense—and accepting its usage—might be a place to start to set new standards.

> *". . . Some women—professional and otherwise—really, really enjoy being treated as sex objects. That really makes it difficult for the rest of us—women and men alike."*

Men often charge that women use sex for their own purposes; i.e., to accomplish business goals or to attract males. Many women also believe this. In a 1987 survey in *Women vs. Women: The Uncivil Business War*, Tara Beth Madden, AMACOM, the question was posed to women across the country: "Have your female co-workers ever felt that some women tend to take advantage of their female attributes to gain business advantages?" Almost 96 percent responded, "yes." Whether the perception is valid or not, women believe it. Using sexual wiles will only reinforce the stereotype. When some use sex as a business tool, others assume that most women do.

Sex is a very real dynamic in an active relationship. Women—and men—do shop for romance in the workplace. Since women and men spend most of their waking hours in the workplace, this process of seeking dates and/or mates by both genders will no doubt continue, no matter how many people moralize otherwise. Women participating in the survey for this book held very divided views on this issue. Although realizing that sexual attraction between co-workers will not stop, most women believe open flirting must. In Scenario 7, Ellen should not have been surprised to find Bob attracted to her when he witnessed her openly flirting with her boss, Joe.

When EEOC and the courts rule on sexual harassment charges, they will consider both participants within the context of their entire behavior, not just the behavior between the alleged offender and alleged offendee. If a woman openly flirts and tells sexually explicit jokes, the agencies and courts will not bend over backwards to protect her from males who give her the same treatment. Thus, both women and men must learn to put sex on hold until after work. The proper place for an expression of this attraction is not the workplace. If the attraction stops, women must learn how to say "no," and men must learn what "no" means.

While women must curb some of these negative behaviors, they may/must also incorporate some positive behaviors. As stated earlier, people accept change when they see a new world vision. If women wish equal opportunity, equal pay and treatment with respect, they must visualize themselves in a new world order that they create. Women must be proactive to effect change.

> *". . . If the situation did not improve, I would quit and contact the EEO."*

Comments from many of the respondents showed women's willingness to speak up when demeaned, insulted or merely annoyed. If men are to change, women must continue to tell them when their behavior is unacceptable and why. How one confronts others depends upon the situation. The range of options is wide. If a woman is angry, she may and should show that. Why keep it locked inside? *Nice girls* can use anger, just as men have done, when appropriate. A dose of anger fired in the right direction might stop bodily contact and/or real crudity. However, the more women can use finesse, the farther along they will be in building relationships. Practicing and using an appropriate retort for most occasions, to be stated in a calm voice, might be a good investment; i.e., "That really offends me because..." This does not direct blame at the attacker, but it gives that individual the message.

One woman, referring to the porno party at the hotel, which was not a bonding experience, stated, "Although I would not go any further with this information, it would certainly change my feeling about the company." If women expect managements to change, women must share these feelings with senior management. Management alone cannot make changes. They must understand how women think and feel. Women must empower themselves. If the result of speaking out is retaliation, then formal complaints to outside agencies must be lodged. Change is uncomfortable; so change rarely happens unless people are more uncomfortable trying to maintain the status quo than accepting the change. When this happens, they will adjust in order to ease the discomfort. Women must raise the discomfort level prudently to bring about the new world order.

Of greatest importance, women must learn the word *unwelcome*. To stop sexual harassment and, if necessary, complain for assistance in getting it stopped, women must tell their harassers and their managements that the attention is "unwelcome." Without that, managements, agencies and courts of law will not respond. Women must learn to speak up.

MALE BEHAVIOR

Most of this book has focused on women, suggesting desired changes in male behavior in response to the Ninth Circuit Court's decision to view harassment through the "eyes of the victim." Men are also victims, and the law will treat them similarly, protecting them from women's harassing behaviors. As the past pages support, no one, regardless of sex, has the license to act without respect for fellow human beings.

The accomplishment of mutual respect, however, presents a great challenge, since past practices are highly ingrained and many men do not understand how or why their behaviors are offensive. The law mandates change; men must comply. If, however, they learn to understand how and why their behaviors are offensive, they will find it far easier to change such behaviors. It would be easy to look at men stereotypically, but each man is inherently unique. Men today, just as women, are in various stages of growth and development . . . various stages of acceptance of women in professional, mixed-gender relationships . . . various stages of respect for all individuals, regardless of sex, race, age or religion.

Many men do not like the "men's club," but they don't know how to change the staus quo. It is likely that as many men as women are offended and embarrassed by nudes on cakes and girlie pictures on walls. The question is: What can they do about it? Today, the law gives them a mouthpiece. Suggestions can be brought forth to management with less individual stigma than before. Hopefully, men will speak up about serious concerns. Hopefully the "men's club" will diminish in importance as more men publicly praise good ideas from both genders.

"Tact is not male/female."

Men as well as women wrestle with their gender roles. Women are claiming both the right and repsonsibility for some "breadwinning," and not always by choice. Men must come to grips with their own changing male roles as well as the need for women to hold positions of responsibility. They must see themselves as equal partners, not dominant; they must give not only economic but emotional support to women, assistance both in the workplace and on the homefront. The world has changed; it will not go back to yesterday.

Men must learn to react positively to feedback from women, however strident, and learn to tell women when their behaviors or dress offends them. They can do this by using their thinking skills, their assessing skills; by reflecting on real experiences with women rather than falling back on stereotypes and perceptions from the past; by understanding that women are also learning, making mistakes, finding that "being just like men" at work will not lead to success; by understanding that women will no longer take insults, degradation or unequal treatment.

Fortunately, role models for this behavior lie within the confines of every workplace—sincere, caring men who treat women with respect every day. Men in need of new behaviors might look around them to find men who model behavior that meets the demands of the law.

From there, they can proceed to examine their own interactions with women, analyze the behavior of women, talk to women and ask them what offends them, apologize when they have made a mistake in judgement or have misread an individual.

If men—and women—meet this challenge, respect for all individuals in the workplace will grow and flourish. Respect comes with understanding and accepting the autonomy of another individual—allowing each individual to be herself or himself.

Respect

Respect is earned, not given. Yet, respect is rarely possible without understanding. Thus, knowing oneself and others begets the possibility of respect if it is earned. Don Thoren, a Phoenix, Arizona based business consultant, advises in his Managing Joint Productivity Workshop: "I will learn how to help other people in ways that enable them to understand me better and improve our joint results."

To gain individual respect for each other, women and men must learn to respond to each other's individual comfort zone, presented in Chapter 3. To do this, it is necessary to apply the 3 R's—learning to read, respect and respond to each other's individual comfort zones.

Reading is not that difficult. If a man who is working with and around a woman will closely observe her behavior, this behavior will provide him with many cues about how she wishes him to treat her. For example, if she pats him on the back, then patting her on the back is okay. This would apply to a two-fisted handshake, a hug or an occasional four-letter word. However, if a man observes that a woman maintains greater than average distance, then he is advised not to touch or stand too close.

Learning to read also includes sharpening one's perception skills: differentiating between what people mean versus what they say or how they act; picking up non-verbal messages from others; sensing delicate or difficult situations; drawing accurate conclusions from ambiguous/confusing situations; anticipating moods of co-workers. In short, being aware of the behavior of others.

Respecting deals with the consequences of how one interacts with a woman's comfort zone. If one disregards or does not respect a woman's comfort zone, the negative potential is a charge of harassment or litigation. Thinking through"if I stand too close or touch her, she'll scream harassment . . . so, I'd better keep my distance" has positive potential consequences that can result in joint productivity and increased harmony in the workplace.

Responding often requires values and beliefs to change—in this case, values and beliefs about women. Values, held at a deep emotional level, are the viewpoint one has based upon years of social conditioning. Beliefs are conclusions from one's own personal experience and are more rational or cognitive.

"Professional treatment is usually the result of professional behavior."

Men tend to have a lot of values about women, mainly from stereotypes as discussed previously. When men learn to read and respect women, their prejudices are soon replaced by beliefs based on experiences rather than values accepted from the past. This change then allows them to respond and build relationships based upon mutual respect.

DESIGNING THE NEW WORKPLACE

Today, women and men are interdependent with equal status. In marriage, women and men work toward common goals for the family. So too in the workforce, women and men must work toward common goals. Regardless of whether this work is personal or professional, the changing balance is an equal partnership rather than a dominant/subordinate (normally sexually defined) relationship. Building these equal partnerships requires a building of respect. To do that, women and men must become friends not foes.

For this to happen, both genders must re-think how they interact. New rules must emerge to assist a different process of relationship building. But, before rules are designed, the new workplace must be designed. What, in fact do the employees want the workplace to be? Will it be a collection of robots who spend eight or more hours a day without anyone ever knowing them; i.e., never discussing their personal lives? Should no one ever mention they are going to have a baby, or spend their vacation in Florida? Is it best not to show pictures of major events? Or, should the workplace be a place that will fulfill some social needs? All human beings have social needs. Should such needs be deprived for the major part of people's waking hours, in order to avoid offending or being offended? No one has suggested going to work in sackcloth and ashes. Attractiveness is not evil, nor is good grooming or good taste in clothes. If human beings wish to share normal discourse in their daily lives, they must rewrite the rules. Equal partnership responses must be allowed to emerge, without impeding the rights of others.

Examples from some of the scenarios will portray the problems. In Scenario 16, most women went willingly to work in the home of a male co-worker to design a training program. This was a daytime event *chaperoned* by his wife. Yet, if men and women are professional friends, building a relationship based upon mutual trust and friendship, they should be able to trust each other and accept a ride home, as in Scenario 46 or a walk home, as in Scenario 26, from a Christmas party, without a man believing a woman is sexually interested in him or the outside world finding it offensive. Men and women are now travelling together on business; should a woman decline dinner and a walk around the neighborhood of the hotel where they are staying if both of them want exercise? If visiting managers ask the temporary secretary what's going on in town, must she say, "I have no idea," and glue her forehead to her desk? Voting on the scenarios shows women as well as men are uncertain as to the answers.

"Tell him I value his friendship and don't want to mess the relationship up."

Women are friendly. Often, a woman looks a man in the eye when he speaks. Does that lead him to believe she is seriously interested in romance rather than a career discussion? Did that lead a gentleman to believe he might be welcome following a walk home from the Christmas party? Or, is there a need to understand the differences between female and male behavior? Should anyone be allowed to make a mistake? In discussing the walk home from the Christmas party, one woman commented: "He made a mistake. Men as well as women can make mistakes." In looking at the temporary secretary who "mouthed off" in the elevator about her bosses with "mid-life crises," one woman responded: "Ellen should have been more specific than labeling 'mid-life crisis,' however, the Personnel Manager's retort was completely unfair." Granted, Ellen's comments were not well thought out. Granted, she made a mistake. How much should individuals be penalized for their mistakes?

To become human beings in the fullest sense, compassion must be shown. It is gratifying that so many women accepted the vice president's condolences and the arm around the shoulder that she needed at the time! Learning to read, respect and respond to each other's comfort zones will help the process of building mixed-gender relationships.

Some environments will be more difficult than others to change. The challenge in changing male-dominated environments is starkly obvious. But, it must be met. Women must be attracted into male-dominated environments if they are to meet the challenge of global competition with talented and trained resources. Behavioral changes must be mandated and an attempt must be made to sensitize men to the thoughts and feelings of women.

Building on a Base

Most of the news in this book has been disconcerting! But, isn't that what makes it news? The *nice guys* don't always make the front pages of the newspaper. But, in looking outward, the nice guys make up far more of the population than the individuals presented in most of the scenarios. Every day, outstanding managers of both genders grow both profits and individuals subordinate to them. Every day, same sex and mixed-gender relationships grow in organizations across the country, even across the world. People helping people. This is the base on which to build. Losing sight of this would be disastrous.

"It's difficult to bond when you're excluded and degraded."

Mentoring—developing proteges—has helped a wide variety of individuals of both genders in different industries. This can be apprenticeship programs or on-the-job training in manufacturing plants, PC gurus sharing programs and expertise or managers hand-picking proteges with potential and moving them along with daily advice and counsel. Mentoring, sharing, growing; that's building on a base. No one must lose sight of the need for that and inadvertently throw it out because it has screened out minorities and women in the past. The challenge is to expand this mentoring to more minorities and women—to select proteges with closer scrutiny. If the *old boy network* continues to select the next *old boy network*, too much talent will fall between the cracks. Perhaps outside consultants can be more objective about determining real talent and potential skill levels of individuals within organizations who have not yet had the opportunity to demonstrate them in-house; a new philosophy of management succession.

As more senior members of organizations raise daughters, pay for college tuitions, and then see their daughters in professional roles, they will face new information. When a father discusses his medical condition with his physician daughter, he will slowly understand the extent of her capabilities. When a daughter works side by side with her father gutting her family room walls and rebuilding them, he will begin to learn that she is capable of not only "heavy work" but also quality craftsmanship. Organizations wishing to promote new respect must tap the real experiences of their members, not old stereotypes, to help change attitudes. Change must build upon new awareness of change.

"Not only did he assure her his wife would be there, he offered lunch also. Gotta like the guy."

Mixed-gender relationships work. Sexual attraction may come into play. Mature employees must learn to work out these situations. Management will not assist in growing individuals into mixed-gender teams if it rushes in uninvited and separates individuals because they have exchanged some sparks, past or present. If employees are to grow and develop the skills of handling problems during this *learning to build phase*, then managements must allow them to learn unless they ask for assistance or create business problems. As individuals become skilled, the base on which respect is built will continue to grow with renewed faith in human beings.

Chapter Six

Meeting the Challenge with Programs and Training:
The Authors' Advice

Respect is earned. Not only must employees earn respect by learning to respect each other, but employers must also provide a climate in which that respect can flourish. Three factors demand this. First, today we understand that no one need live in oppression, whether in foreign countries with different philosophies from ours, or in the United States. If we truly believe that we are all *created equal*, then our own humanity requires giving each other the right to authenticity. Second, individual businesses are learning that to become and remain profitable requires retraining talented people and using all their ideas. Third, America's global competitiveness demands that mixed-gender and mixed-racial relationships work to accomplish organizational goals. Thus, we must end discrimination and harassment *in all forms*.

The Equal Employment Opportunity Commission guidelines state that prevention is the best tool to eliminate sexual harassment. Prevention requires creation of a specific program, specific policies and specific training.

The Program

Company Philosophy: Determine a company philosophy and state it publicly to employees; strongly disapprove of harassing actions.

The Policy: Create and maintain a policy, separate from policies regarding general employment concerns, that describes the company philosophy and states internal processes for investigation and sanction of offenders.

Internal Processes: Establish internal processes for victims to state concerns or charges; such grievance procedures must be fair, confidential within the boundaries of investigation mandated by law and conducted in a timely manner. Provide an alternate route around the employee's direct supervisor for instances where the supervisor is the alleged offender or the alleged victim is not comfortable discussing the topic with him/her.

Claims Review: Investigate claims and report your findings to the individuals involved in a timely manner.

Communication: Disseminate the policy within a communication plan that includes:
- educating employees about sexual harassment so that they fully understand *quid pro quo, hostile work environment, unwelcome behavior;* employer sanctions; EEOC's role and the views of the courts.
- educating employees about internal processes; ensuring understanding of how to raise the issue of harassment and what to expect.
- informing all employees of their rights as offenders and/or victims.

Maintenance: Develop a plan to monitor those managers who do not follow company philosophy and/or retaliate against employees who share concerns or process grievances. Encourage employees to report sexual harassment claims.

Training: Provide thorough training, guidance and ongoing counseling of managers; ensure that they understand their own and the organization's liability for harassment, which they allow by failing to take immediate action. Provide sensitivity training to all employees to promote desired behavior changes and build mixed-gender, mixed-racial relationships.

A PROGRAM WITH TEETH—OR LIP SERVICE? A CHECKLIST

Express Strong Disapproval

An organization's policy condemning sexual harassment may meet the *letter of the law*. But, if it does not meet the *spirit of the law*, the first step is to admit it. If an organization does not find sexual harassment in its workplace, it is not looking deep enough. Sexual harassment pervades every workplace. An employee survey or an employee audit will reveal its extent. Once understood, reinforcement and monitoring of sanctions must follow. When employees see these in practice, they will understand that management disapproves strongly.

Provide Appropriate Sanctions

No longer is it enough to mildly scold the harasser and move the harassee to another job. By law, the victim must not be moved from the job. When blatant harassment is labeled as *horseplay*, or *boys will be boys*, agencies and courts will disagree with management. Managements must stop sexual harassment. Actions speak louder than words. Treating offenders with serious disciplinary measures will protect the organization and its employees.

Inform Employees of Their Rights

The *head in the sand approach* will not work today. EEOC has mandated educating employees fully. Women understand harassment, with or without an employer's assistance. When management is viewed as *user unfriendly*, victims will seek assistance outside.

Smugness! Complacency! Lack of awareness of sexual harassment issues! These are normal reactions of organizations that believe "sexual harassment happens down the street, not here. Besides, we have a policy against it." Organizations of this ilk are ripe for trouble. EEOC bluntly addresses employers such as these with the words, "sensitize all employees." Begin with a needs assessment to determine what is tolerated in your workplace versus healthy, appropriate behavior. Ferret out unreported harassment.

Sensitize All Employees

Develop training solutions. Train managers first. If they do not understand precisely what is and isn't harassment, how women think and feel and what to expect from their potential victims, they will never create a workplace free from harassment. Then, move on to training employees. Through well-designed training, taken seriously by management, not only will harassment lessen, employees will understand that management really cares.

Respond to Employee Needs

Just as organizations have begun to understand the needs of customers and stockholders, they must also understand the needs of employees within the framework of the total business. It may take several years to sensitize management to employee needs. In the interim, select an Ombudsperson, separate from management or human resources, to respond to complaints. Or, allow employees to complain to any member of management, or the company nurse. Flexibility may well accomplish the dual goal of responding to employee needs and protecting the business. The test of your responsiveness is—is it easier for an employee of yours to call EEOC or a lawyer than to solve their problems internally? Responding to employee needs means providing internal support.

Respond Immediately

Understand that as soon as a complaint is made to anyone in management, your organization is on notice. The law states that you must respond. You must stop the harassment, hold an investigation, and sanction the offender(s), if you believe them to be guilty. Not all alleged offenders are guilty; often misunderstandings occur. Sometimes, simply telling an employee to back off may solve the problem before it escalates into a formal case under agency or legal review.

Overturn Age-Old Management Maxims

If managers in your organization allow harassment to continue unpunished, do not back them. Managers are not always right. If managers believe the adage, "If it ain't broke, don't fix it," they may lose sight of one strong legal mandate. They are bound legally not only by what they know, but also by what they should have known.

Managers who hide in their offices or put their heads in the sand will not protect your organization. If you hope to build employee trust and global competitiveness, you must grow your current managers for this era, or replace them.

Assess the Costs

Like the lube ad says, "Pay now, or pay later." The cost of training becomes miniscule in comparison with the cost of litigation and fines.

Provide Commitment

Everything stems from the top. No one will believe your organization is committed to preventing sexual harassment unless top management believes in it and manifests that belief concretely—by underwriting fairness to all employees. Management can start by issuing a policy. (This need not be long; if you keep it to the essentials and it is well-written, it might even fit on one page!)

The Policy

Company Philosophy: Include within a total quality of worklife, but be specific regarding sexual harassment within this.

Definitions: Define harassment and hostile work environment, as mandated by law. Ensure that employees know you will not condone these behaviors.

Processes: Identify the system to voice complaints and ask for investigation. Provide just enough detail to be understood, but not so much that it cannot be practiced with consistency.

Alternatives: Define any alternate processes that can be used if the above-stated process is inapppropriate; i.e., other members of management or an ombudsperson.

Training

Sexual harassment is gray—not just black and white. Harassment must be seen from the eyes of *a reasonable woman*. This subjectivity requires a specific type of training that includes understanding the world through someone else's eyes. When training managers or employees, role playing, videos and reading that allow employees to understand examples of sexual harassment, succeed best. If either group does not understand what constitutes harassing behavior, they can hardly be expected to stop it. No one likes to be told, "Do it because I (or the law) says so without understanding why." Training must also include understanding of the internal system to file complaints and request investigations. Without a system that works, harassment will not be contained.

Beyond this, managers must understand their responsibilities: how to spot problems, what to do when someone approaches them, appropriate sanctions they must mete out. If they don't, they will not prevent sexual harassment. And so, managers require training beyond that given to employees.

For all employees, managers and individual contributors, small group meetings produce top results. They allow individuals to spend time on the subtleties, to understand the gray areas when they can't fall back on the black and white. Emotionally they involve themselves in the process in smaller group meetings. However, if that is not possible initially, the authors advise training en masse and working on regrouping later in smaller groups.

Three critical factors stand out:

- The *reasonable woman standard* mandates that harassment be determined by the victim's point of view. Training must provide that perspective.
- Training must be timely given the new legislation and landmark cases of 1991.
- Attendance at training should be documented to protect the organization from further claims should harassment charges be leveled and/or proven.

Investigation of Charges

Investigation of charges is the meat of the program. Sometimes employees withdraw complaints after discussing them with management, realizing the advantages of handling situations directly with the offending party. The law, however, mandates an investigation of any formal accusations. An investigation should include a detailed interview with the victim to determine:

- Who, what, when (how often), where, how the harassment occurred, and hopefully, why.

- How the victim felt about the incident. What was the victim's response? Was the harasser advised that the action was unwelcome? Were there any witnesses?
- If the victim told anyone. Does the victim believe there may be other victims? If so, could information be discreetly obtained about other incidents?
- What the victim would like to have done.

The investigator must then decide if the complaint warrants emergency action or informal resolution, how the individuals involved and company should be protected, and set a course of action to prove or disprove the charge by discussion with the alleged offender.

When determining how to investigate charges, several main points were shared by Deborah Gage Haude, labor and employment relations litigator from the Chicago law firm of Winston and Strawn:

- Who will perform the investigation? While a woman may be preferable, a good listener is necessary.
- Do not trivialize the charge or either party.
- While it is important to document the facts, it is even more important to make the individual comfortable first so that all the facts will come out. When the facts have been heard, determine the seriousness of the complaint. Rushing in too fast to document the complaint "for the record" may only exacerbate a minor situation.
- A goal should be to assist an employee who believes that he/she has been harassed in feeling that they are in control of themselves and their environments. This is good for the company and good for the person.
- Remember: you have a business to run. Prevent rumors. Keep it reasonably confidential. But, make sure the alleged victim understands you must do an investigation.

Sometimes a solution becomes obvious and the victim takes responsibility for resolving the complaint on her/his own. That's what Deborah Gage Haude talked about—assisting the victim in taking back control of the environment. If that cannot be accomplished, then the complaint should be documented and investigated, using both hearsay and documents; i.e., personnel files, witnessed past behavior of both participants, to piece together where the truth lies. As much confidentiality as possible must be maintained, but complaints cannot be investigated without asking potential witnesses, other employees who may have experienced similar situations and the alleged offender. The investigation must determine if the action was unwelcome at the time. Using sensitivity and urging confidentiality on the part of all individuals involved is important.

During the investigation, the alleged victim must not suffer. Temporary measures must be put in place if the charge is serious enough. When the investigation is finished, the investigator must tell the alleged victim of the results and any sanctions placed on any individual. The victim must not be penalized; she/he must not be removed from the position or transferred. The company must ensure that no retaliation toward the victim will occur.

MEETING THE CHALLENGE

We cannot start too soon. We can stop harassment; we can stop discrimination. But, in order to attract women into occupations needed for America to be competitive we must move programs downward into pre-school and elementary school classrooms. Girls must be encouraged to become serious students of math and science and given an opportunity to understand technology as a designer, not just a user. They need classroom attention; they need career counseling that presents a wider range of opportunities.

Young girls need competitive sports programs. Women who participate in competitive sports throughout their lives have learned different behaviors than their less competitive sisters: how to work with *guys* and become part of a team, how not to whine or complain, how to play hard and aggressively while understanding that you can't win them all. They learn to handle stress situations, which helps when making presentations to top management when needed. They learn early in life that they can survive and compete. They learn not to take failure personally. Confidence sets them apart. In order to fully utilize the talents of women, programs must be put in place to help them early in life to build confidence, skills and a different intellectual base.

We must learn to respect each other for many reasons. In short, harassment is waste: human waste, talent waste, dollar waste! These are costs to everyone's bottom line, as they impact emotions and well beings as well as economics. Both harmony and use of everyone's talents are needed to move us forward. It would be noble to say that to ensure a sane society we can no longer allow harassment to continue. Important as this is, however, additional concerns exist. To survive economically, harassing behavior must be stopped and replaced with respect.

A Young Woman's
Scenario of Hope . . .

ONE WOMAN'S VIEW: CAN'T WE LEARN JUST TO BE HUMAN BEINGS?

Following are excerpts from a lengthy interview with one woman working on being herself and being a human being amidst the issues of her era:

I'm not sure why I've always worked in jobs where men held power, but I have. I started working as a waitress for a short guy with a need to build his macho image. He made a lot of sexual inferences toward me, but I'm not sure that was because they were sexually motivated or because he was just asserting his power. I tend to think the latter. He was probably a jerk toward other men so I didn't take it personally. I've generally had good luck in the restaurant and bar businesses.

I had a waitressing job where one guy would make comments whenever I went to the back room to make the ice cream. He would ask if "I would come over to his house and put whipped cream on his ice cream or something else." I ended up walking off that job. I was too young to realize I had the right to walk into the manager's office and say, "Hey, this guy is making these comments and I don't want to listen to them."

• • •

In working construction I went behind a group of guys who inset windows and I did the staining and painting. Sometimes I actually inset the windows and also did carpentry. There were always comments made; comments about my breasts. One day one guy grabbed my breasts and I turned around and knocked off his hat. I started laughing. He was bald. He was so embarrassed, he just walked away. After that the issue was not dealt with. Otherwise, I

have not had problems with construction guys abusing me sexually—comments, yes, millions and millions of comments. This is so
normal in general conversation in construction. It's barroom talk.
While they don't mean anything by it, I feel it's not necessary. I feel
there would be a lot of women in this country who would say,
"That's out of line and not necessary," and they probably should
get up and say that.

I had a boss who was upset about a business issue. He walked off
the site with me to the trailer and said, "I'm going to the bathroom
and piss some of this tension out of me." I said, "Okay." As we
walked, the discussion moved to masseuses and hookers. We
talked about the profession. He acknowledged that I would not be
a good hooker at all. Was that sexual harassment? I thought he had
given me a compliment. Ninety-nine percent of the women in your
survey would probably say all these comments were uncalled for,
and may have cried "sexual harassment." The fact is, it wasn't
directed at me. He didn't even look at me. He was stressed out. He
was just spouting. He was just being a normal human being.

· · ·

A friend in construction didn't like the comments and she started
a BWA Club, "Butt Watchers of America," and started making
retaliatory comments, such as, "What do you think? His butt's
better or not?" I'm not so sure that's the answer. In fact, I'm sure it's
not. If I am a reasonable woman, neither of these is acceptable. But
the point that must be addressed in your book is: are we no longer
going to be human beings? If I'm so clumsy some day that I drop
anything I touch, can I say "It's PMS, I know it is." I wouldn't like
a male to say that to me, however. It would be an insinuation. But,
can't we let off tension building up inside of us without worrying
about (a) being sued, (b) losing our jobs, (3) not being human
beings? *I mean can we no longer be human beings?*

· · ·

I really wanted to make it in the film business. My studies, my
degree from college, my years of watching old movies and com-
mercials—in fact my whole life was spent in film! But, the film
business is where I encountered *real* sexual harassment. Every time
I walked on a set, unless those people specifically knew me,
someone would say, "Makeup's that way sweetheart!" After a
while I got so tired of it I would just blurt out, "Listen you son of a
bitch, I'm the producer here and I want to know what's going on,
not where makeup is!" I had to assert myself with that tone to get
someone to understand I was not a bimbo hanging around the set

looking for work. I was there for business. For that reason alone after my third year working on the sets I changed my look. I cut off my hair, changed my clothing. I said, "No more." I had bought into it hook, line and sinker that in the film business you had to have an image, you had to be this big, sexy, red-hot mama. I started wearing conservative clothes, no makeup. I didn't try to be fun, to be myself. I lost jobs.

That was the point at which I got out of the business. I didn't want to get out, but I was just sick and tired of it. I was tired of directors knocking on my hotel room doors at midnight after 14 hour shoots asking me to go with them for a drink. It would have been different if it were a buddy of mine that I worked with in the business that wanted to talk about his girlfriend or his life, or just have a drink and unwind. But my friends were asleep by then, and so was I. I didn't appreciated being awakened at that hour!

I didn't sleep with anyone in the film business. As long as I looked sexy I kept getting jobs. It was the pursuit. Let's hire her back. Maybe I can get her in bed. A constant issue. It took too much out of me. Watching the guys come down on me. You can always tell them. They look like wolves when they come down. When anyone is putting that kind of pressure on you, it's definitely sexual harassment. With these issues I did not feel comfortable. So I finally left the business. Film is mostly freelance—they can call you or not. Nobody owns the workplace. You can't spend your life fighting.

• • •

I'm not a special woman just because I'm slightly attractive. I used to think that was it. But, if a guy is going to do that to me he is going to do that to others. There are lots of guys out there who don't; lots of guys who treat you with total respect. They never give you comments. We talk about all kinds of issues, some of them might be construed as sexual in nature, but they aren't sexual situations. They might be discussions about sexual subjects, intellectual discussions. Can't we do that? Can't we learn to share ideas? Can't we learn to be friends? Can't we listen to each other? *Can't we just learn to be human beings?*

• • •

I'm back in construction. It's steady work at the moment, but not for long. I've always wanted to prove that I could deal with it But, I don't have to prove it anymore. I just have to get on with my life—find a job or a career that I like where I can be myself, have fun and contribute something worthwhile. But, there's a recession out there . . . .

• • •

We women have been screaming and shouting in stages of denial
—of our rights and ourselves for a long time. Since the 1960s, we
have gone through anger, which has broken up families and
cultural centers. The basis is our sexuality and how it has been
abused. We manifest ourselves in every arena as we display our
anger.

Now we are ready for a healing phase, an empowerment, a
standing up for ourselves. We face power harassment that exists in
dark shadows. You drop a rock in the water and all kinds of ripples
occur. When this happens, we must say, "I find your behavior
unacceptable" in a healing mode, moving away from anger and
blame. We must show respect for ourselves as women. When we
lack respect for ourselves, we cannot respect others or expect others
to respect us.

Today, women are in healing. They are standing up for themselves
and will continue to do so. I have spent too many years standing up
for myself without concern for the other person. Now I finally
realize how important that is. We will lead the way to a higher plane
of life. If we do not heal and help others to heal, our planet will not
survive.